Dog
Walk
Talk

Dog
Walk
Talk

While I'm Walking, God's Talking

Joe Miller

XULON PRESS ELITE

Xulon Press Elite
2301 Lucien Way #415
Maitland, FL 32751
407.339.4217
www.xulonpress.com

© 2020 by Joe Miller

Cover photography by Morgan Kukovek, MK Photography, Hampshire, IL

Printed in the United States of America.

Paperback ISBN-13: 978-1-6312-9554-6
Ebook ISBN-13: 978-1-6312-9555-3

Outside of a dog, a book is man's best friend.
Inside of a dog, it's too dark to read.
~ Groucho Marx[1]

FOREWORD

The first time I met Joe was at a men's weekend dedicated to spiritual growth. I had the opportunity to witness a significant outpouring of God's grace, truth, and love in his life. It was a memorable moment. What struck me most about Joe was his openness and authenticity as he took the risk to meet God in a deep way. It not only impacted him, but his story and encounter with God helped to create an environment of vulnerability and receptivity to God's Spirit among all who were present. Each time I have been with Joe since then has been an encounter with his big heart and, of course, a good dash of humor. *Dog Walk Talk* is a genuine expression of who Joe is—relatable, big-hearted, honest, authentic, and dedicated to living a life pleasing to God. His willingness to be real inspires others to do the same. He touches on key life issues and concerns, offering the hope that God is right there with us in and through it all. As you read, take it slow and allow God to bring to your awareness your own story and how He desires to meet you there. This is a walk that you don't want to rush.

~ **Bob Hudson,** Denver, Colorado, February 19, 2020

Bob is the Founder of The Cross Ministry Group, as well as the Men at the Cross and Women at the Cross weekend retreats. He has created multiple seminars for men and women, which include Living in Truth, Breaking Down the Walls, and a series dealing with loving God with all our Heart, Soul, Mind, and Strength. Bob holds a Master of Divinity from Gordon-Conwell Theological Seminary in South Hamilton, MA, and a Master of Art in Counseling from Denver Seminary in Denver, Colorado.

This book need not be thought of as a page-turner, but perhaps as a nightstand book, a coffee table book, or the best use—a book to be used while in your favorite quiet time space. After all, it's not a story—it's real life. I hope you will enjoy the random topics as they come. You may be surprised. As you journey through this book, you may find your best friends are highlighters, pens, or pencils for making notes or underlining; fingers to bend a corner of a page for future reference; and, of course, the mother lode of any serious reader—a pack of Post-It notes™. Have at it—it's your book and, perhaps, just a bit of your life!

Warm regards,
Your unconventional author, Joe Miller

TABLE OF CONTENTS

INTRODUCTION

Dog Walk Talk

(While I'm walking, God's talking)

W hy is it called *Dog Walk Talk*? I have never met a person who just cruised blindly and without question through life. We all think about things, and most of us think about life, its meaning, our place in it, and our destiny. Some of us do our best introspective thinking while in meditation or in quiet times. Others find that being in nature opens the doors to mind and heart. Still, others may find a depth of introspection while listening to music or perhaps simply while in the shower. It varies with each of us and may encompass several different settings. I have found that my best thinking and ability to hear God's still voice most often occurs while walking my dog out in nature. I have often been reminded that "dog" is "God" spelled backwards.

Dog Walk Talk is a collection of thought-provoking, biblical-ly-thought-through anecdotes which focus on some of the issues, thoughts, actions, and dilemmas we all face as we hike our spiritual journey, whether we are just curious about this God thing, somewhat participating in it, or fully enmeshed in our walk. We are on that hike to help us to draw closer to God and be better people as a result. There are no gender or age limits to the purpose of these writings.

Through these short personal anecdotes that look at life through a filter other than the worldview and that speak to my personal walk from a life of messiness to a life of improved and ongoing spiritual maturity, I hope readers can find some thought-producing insights that touch their own spiritual journeys.

On these pages, I share some of my life and a bit of other's lives with you. They are lives of ups and downs, goods and not-so-goods, laughter and tears, and often some messes. Not always an easy share. I pray that both Christ-following and non-believing readers can relate to the "been there, done that" moments in these pages, as well as to some of my musings about the struggles of life in general. I think it is safe to say we've all been there, or we may be there at present. Each reflection ends with thought-provoking, perhaps challenging, questions and Scripture references to biblically validate what you have read and provide for further thought and study.

For the Christ-follower, you are likely as grateful as I am for God's role in all of life's circumstances.

For the non-believer...well, you will perhaps sometimes grit your teeth and make it known that you don't need to read about the God-thing. And so, I gently plead my case before you. I ask that you consider my words of challenge in the What About You segments of the readings. Maybe grab a Bible (if not in hard copy, I'm guessing you know how to do an online search), hit the Table of Contents to help you find the Encouraging Words verses I've listed, and take a few seconds to read them. The verses may or may not speak to you. Reality is some parts of the Bible are difficult to understand and/or we immediately reject them as "that doesn't apply to me." But, by reading the suggested verses in their context, I believe God will plant something in your heart. That something may not make a difference immediately, maybe not ever, but I'm confident you will carry those words you read into the next days, weeks, or years of your life.

My hope is that each of you who read the pages of this book will be better equipped to <u>live your eulogy</u> as you are brought to see reflections of yourself in the writings. The intent of the book is to offer topics which can stir the reader to contemplate how an article speaks to their heart. These life lessons are offered to promote honest self-examination, to provide an opportunity to reflect on those examinations, and to give scriptural proof for godly conclusions. I pray that the result will be in the form of self-discovered change, change that can help you become a godlier person as you do this thing called life.

Wherever in life you are, or whoever you are as a reader of my writings, if you'd like to connect further with me to share your thoughts or to ask questions, I can be reached at:

E-mail   writesthelyrics@gmail.com
Website   https://www.jbmillerauthor.com
Facebook https://www.facebook.com/authorJoeMiller/

My story is important not because it is mine,
God knows, but because if I tell it anything like right,
the chances are you will recognize that in many ways it is also yours.
It is precisely through these stories that God makes himself
known to each of us more powerfully and personally.
To lose track of our stories is to be profoundly impoverished
not only humanly but spiritually.
~Frederick Buechner[2]

DEDICATION

This book is dedicated to those who aren't yet sure of the awesomeness of our God, the One who loves all of us, the One who says to every person, "You matter to Me," and "You are a beloved child of Mine *no matter what or where you're at in your life.*"

It's also dedicated to my dad:

I Never Really Knew You

I'm sorry, Dad, deeply sorry. I hope that somehow you know what I'm writing. You died many years ago. I wasn't there. Just as I wasn't there during much of our time on earth together. You tried. You wanted a relationship. I see that now. I also see that I was the one that turned my back on it. I was respectful, perhaps out of fear, but I thought of you as an old fuddy-duddy—one out of touch with what was happening in my own little world. I was too busy for you.

I remember some small splotches of my early youth and can see you as a loving, happy, and interested daddy, even with all that was going on with Mom and Sis. But those memories are few and clouded. I mainly see the teen and young-man years of mine when you still wanted to be "the dad," but I was somewhere else—detached, uninterested, and mostly uncaring.

I remember later visits with you and Mom, obligatory visits so you could see the kids and hear me brag about how well I was doing. And I remember on those visits, when you were medically retired, how I found every excuse in the world to avoid just taking the time to sit and talk with you—something you obviously wanted in those waning years of yours. You never gave up hope, but I could see the hurt in your eyes, and I ignored it.

Then you died, and once again, I wasn't there. I never really knew you, Dad, because I didn't make the effort or take the time. And now I am sorry—for both of us. You gave it your best shot; I gave it my worst. And I lost something—special memories of a relationship with a good dad.

Things have changed now. I'm not who I was. I am a new man, one with a relationship with Jesus, the One who has taught me how important earthly relationships are to be. He's the same Jesus you had a relationship with. Only, I just didn't get it then. You saw the mess and never got the chance to see the maturity. Forgive me, Dad, you sure tried and now I see it.

Until I get there...

ACKNOWLEDGEMENTS

K elly, Duke, Trotter, Zeus, and the first Kelly. Each of them, one of my kids—but with four legs and a wagging tail. They were the dogs that allowed me to walk them in places where I could be free for a while and think about life and how I fit in it. Each of them showed the same characteristics that God has consistently shown me (and shows all of us, if we would only see them):

- ✓ Never-ending faithfulness
- ✓ Unconditional love
- ✓ Total acceptance
- ✓ Endless grace
- ✓ An unfailing desire for my heart

Thank you, boy and girl canines, for taking this old man on the journey into his heart and mind as you walked patiently by his side down by the river, on the trails, and out in the woods. You gave me much more than I could ever give you in return.

I cannot give enough thanks to the guys in my small group. They loved me through some hard times, accepted me as I was and reeled me back in when I needed it. Compassionate, yet tough, their transparency set the bar for my own developing openness.

Some of the strongest moral support in my times of doubt came from a friend of six-decades, Bill Ronay. Though fighting the cancer which eventually took him, he walked without complaint and with dignity alongside me as I shared my struggles to write some of these difficult musings. He also provided me with an invaluable example of how to face death with grace. He was my brother from another mother. He was a brother who filled me with unconditional love.

Special thanks to a friend who took on the project of proof-reading and editing the pages of the book from inception through to final manuscript, and who diligently and unselfishly provided me with insights where I was lacking them.

Thanks to my wife Penny for putting up with me (and the dogs) through these forty-plus formative years and for allowing me the time and space, aka relational absenteeism, to indulge myself in my creative process. I am pretty sure she could write her own book filled with insights and musings from the wifely and womanly perspective.

ENDORSEMENTS

F ollowing a specific format of diverse examples of human experiences common to all of us, Joe Miller gives us readers valuable
insight into how we can work on ourselves by reading Dog Walk Talk.
The narrative is easy to follow since Mr. Miller applies a prescriptive
format for each topic. Beginning with a quote relevant to the subject
he addresses, he follows by giving us readers a narrative of explanation.
After this, he provides a specific instance where the quote applied to an
event in his life in the segment he titles "About me," followed by asking,
"What about you?" which makes us turn introspective. He allows us, as
his readers, to apply the quote and think about how it applies to an event
or experience in our own lives. Lastly, he leaves a Bible verse to guide us
in our journey to self-awareness and self-improvement.

Many times, in this book, I found myself either connecting with a
similar instance when I felt like he did in my own life or empathizing
with something he went through which I did not. If you're looking for
a self-help book to add to your library that meets every scenario you can
think of that might apply to you, then Joe Miller's *Dog Walk Talk* is a
good investment for your bookshelf. ~ **Carmen Baca:** Carmen taught
a variety of English and history courses at the high school and college
levels over the course of thirty-six years. Her command of both English
and Spanish enables her to write with true story-telling talent. Her
debut novel, *El Hermano,* was published in April of 2017 and became
a finalist in the NM-AZ book awards program. Since 2017, she has published three more books (the fifth publishing this spring) and thirty-five
short works thus far in online literary magazines and anthologies. She

and her husband live a quiet life in the country caring for their animals and any stray that happens to come by.

In *Dog Walk Talk: While I'm Walking, God's Talking,* you will get a glimpse of the man, Joe Miller. Joe is the author of this series of meditations, yes, but like all good authors, he does not leave himself out of the story. Like me, I hope you will discover a man who, even in his seventh decade, is learning to follow wisdom's path after choosing many foolish ones and who is discovering what wholeness looks like on the other side of brokenness. Joe is unafraid to open his life to his readers, and if you give his book a chance, you will be blessed for getting to know a little bit about him. ~ **Jason Kanz:** A husband, father, clinical neuropsychologist, and author of three books: *Soil of the Divine* (2017); *Living in the Larger Story: The Christian Psychology of Larry Crabb* (2019); and *Notes from the Upper Room: Lessons in Loving Like Jesus (2020).*

This is an amazing book that I highly recommend for every Christian. It reads like a conversation with a close friend and speaks right to the heart. I have to say that I've never experienced anything quite like it. The intimate insights and transparency of the author is a refreshing encounter like no other. His willingness to reveal to us (the reader) his own faults and shortcomings, along with the realizations given him during his process of transformation, is truly the epitome of "LOVE THY NEIGHBOR as yourself." If you read only one book this year, THIS should be it! ~ **Victoria Nicodemus,** of Dallas, TX, owns AbideInHope.com and is an acclaimed Web Designer and SEO Consultant for PushLeads.

Joe is an engaging author, using humor, insight, and an incredible transparency that touches the heart. Taking time to ponder the extraordinary thoughts found in the ordinary of daily routine will encourage, strengthen, and uplift with each page turned. ~ **Lance Hurley:** Executive Director, Ignite Church Planting: Chicagoland.

Dog Walk Talk wholeheartedly points us toward God and equips us with the chance to grow in the way we view our Savior. You will appreciate that Joe's style is akin to having a conversation with a dear friend.

Joe's writing speaks honestly to the heart. His stories and analogies allow the reader the opportunity to examine where we truly are in our relationship with God. ~ **Danielle Zapchenk:** As part of the Leadership Team & teaching team of West Ridge Community Church in Elgin, IL, Danielle has a strong and active passion for women's ministry.

This reading caused me to explore my very soul and had me sitting up like a schoolboy at story time. Strongly causes one to self-evaluate, while offering hope in any season. Exceptionally inspiring! Transparent and genuine, playing on the chords of the human spirit. ~ **Joseph Martin Salaiz,** author of *Little Green Plant.*

THE SMILE THAT HIDES ME

I penned the following poem in January of 1992, six years after being witnessed to by a man whose family had disowned him because of his faith and belief in Jesus Christ. At the time of his witness, I was a mess in every aspect of my life. And when I wrote the poem six years into the Christianity thing, I was still a mess (to which my family can attest; some of those memories never fade).

When I pulled out and read the poem these thirty plus years later, I realized that even during my messed-up time, I had written it with a surprisingly deep awareness of self.

- The poem not only indicates awareness, but deep introspection.
- It portrays the struggle between the kid I had been, the guy I was, and the guy I wanted to be.
- Its words paint a picture of being lost, but not without hope.
- It was certainly a cry for help.

It wasn't long after the poem was written that I finally started to "get it." I began to figure out the role God had in store for me. I *started* to feel an appreciation of His grace, and I was beginning to get a grip on what a spiritual life was all about.

If you are experiencing that two-me's feeling, take heart. God has a plan for all of us—yes, you too—even though it may take some time to grasp that plan. I am convinced that we need some life struggles that force us to sort things out so that we can then begin to cross the bridge to spiritual sanity and into spiritual joy.

The Smile That Hides Me
(unedited original version)

My past is deeply within me,
dark and hidden among the trash
of many years of life and its lessons.
It looms and waits; my emotions crash.
I hide all those hidden feelings;
they're buried so deeply within.
Don't prod into the one that's really me,
or I'll break out that cover-up grin.
When my feelings get too near the surface,
it seems that I want to hide.
I'll cover them up in a manner not me;
I'll smile, and I'll smile wide.
Where is that good little boy within
who was once happy and free?
Will you help me discover those feelings?
Let's open the door, you and me.
I've tried all through my life's journey
to blend both body and mind,
to free up that great boy within me,
to discover that which I could find.
Let's open those doors to my mind.
Be kind and gentle, yet strong.
I cower in fear of discovering
all that which I fear is so wrong.
Who is that boy deep within me?
He once knew such joy and was free.
Can he ever break through the barriers
that separate me from me?

Joe Miller ©1-29-92

My hope is that you allow me through my writings to offer my hand, my experiences (good, bad, and ugly), my imperfect wisdom, and my heart in walking alongside you as you maneuver the pathways of life. And you'll see, I've invited God to join us. I can vouch for the fact that He is the best walking partner ever, whether the path is perfectly paved, a bit rocky, or full of potholes. Let's get moving!

May God bless you in your journey.

KELLY REMINDED ME

Let nothing disturb you,
nothing frighten you, all things are passing.
God is unchanging. Patience gains all;
nothing is lacking to those who have God:
God alone is sufficient.
~ St. Teresa of Avila[3]

Dogs can teach us a lot. For eons, they have been referred to as man's best friend. I think God intended it that way. Why else would He have called that four-legged animal, the dog, the reverse of His name? I believe He did so because if we really know dogs, and understand them, they possess infinite qualities that God Himself has. And in seeing those qualities in our relationships with our pooches, we can see God. Abstract thinking? Perhaps. But bear with me.

While walking my dog, Kelly, this morning, I received from her another lesson in godly life as it should be. I contemplated how she never complains, how she takes life in stride, how attentive and devoted she is toward her master, and how satisfied she is with everything in her life. For example, she gets fed the same thing two times a day, 365 days a year. And she drinks water. Just water. She never says that she would rather have table scraps or soft food or perhaps some milk or coffee. Rather, she simply joyously takes her kibble and water. Unlike her human, who must have his steak done just so or who wants orange marmalade instead of grape jelly on his peanut butter sandwich, Kelly is simply and without complaint satisfied with what is dished out for her—without any raised eyebrows or voices in her head decrying something that didn't fulfill her desire.

I marvel in the fact that she is always happy, satisfied with whatever comes her way. If there is a change or an upheaval, she takes it in stride, adapts, and goes on loving us, her masters, without complaint. I thought about how often I am unsatisfied and how unhappy I can get at times. That is when it's all about me—what I can do, what I can get, how I can do it, what I want, what I need. In those times, I forget, or worse, ignore, the fact that my sufficiency is in the Lord—*every single bit of it*. And it is that out of which my sin arises. It's the core root, the feeder root, of the sin within me. Kelly reminds me that all I need to do is faithfully, fully, and unconditionally rely on the Lord for everything about my life—that He will meet my needs, every day, 365 days a year.

Dogs make life seem easy, don't they?

About Me: Shedding my sufficiency and reliance on myself is difficult, as is *fully* relying on the sufficiency of the Lord for my life. I want control yet know that it is in my best interests not to have it. I need only reflect on the many bad decisions I've made over my life to fully grasp that. Unfortunately, my humanness often stands in the way of my quest for godliness and therefore holiness. When I recognize that, I must go to prayer and the Word.

What About You? How do you handle your need for control in your life? Do you struggle with giving in to God and His will? Would your history show a need for contemplative reflection on this issue in your life? When you experience difficult times, know that yielding control to God will bring you a sense of peace and joy. He will never fail you.

Encouraging Words: Proverbs 19:21; Jeremiah 29:11; Matthew 19:26; Philippians 4:6-7

JUST MINUTES

*Grace is the pleasure of God to magnify the worth of God
by giving sinners the right and power to delight
in God without obscuring the glory of God.*
~ John Piper[4]

About Me: How fast those minutes go by, those sixty to seventy-five minutes I spend each Sunday in church. Those are the minutes when my mind consistently and comfortably finds itself in sync with my heart. I sit there not entertained, but in sync with what is going on around me; my soul being touched and massaged with God's outrageous love for me. I find I do not have to be angry at myself for being what and who I am...a broken person. In those minutes I am overwhelmed as I am reminded through music, prayer, community, a message, and communion of the bountiful of the grace which has been given me and the redemption that comes with from that grace. For just those few minutes, I am the me that God made me to be.

But Then it's over.

At times, during the week, sometimes I experience that same beautiful syncing of heart and mind. Often, however, I find myself longing for those in-church minutes because I realize those few precious moments have somehow vanished. I feel cheated that I am not experiencing them. I feel lost. I get sad as I realize that it's all on me. No one took those minutes away. They were there, and they were real, just as God wants; So, then I must admit that I am the culprit. I am the one responsible for putting myself into the positions, times, places, actions, words, situations, habits, practices, and surroundings that allow my heart and mind to sync together as one. If I do not do that consciously and consistently, it's my fault. So, I must ask myself: How do I bring those sixty to seventy-five minutes' in-church emotions to all of my other available minutes?

Those minutes are not just minutes—they are THE minutes. They are the minutes that are glimpses of the me that God wants me to be and that I long to be. They're the minutes when He is whispering to my soul, "This is what it's all about, My son. This is all yours if you want it—if you make the choices. This is how it can be if you really 'get' all that I have shared with you. This is real, and not just minutes. This is life as I meant it to be, as I deem it."

My days are 1,440 minutes long; my weeks, 10,080. That means I'm missing the boat for up to 10,020 minutes a week by not putting those 60 short, yet important, minutes into my life all the time. I have fully come to realize they're not just minutes, but they are real life as God intends for it to be.

What About You? What are the times you most feel the sync between your mind and heart? Do you cherish those moments? Do you feel the presence of God in those moments, or does worldliness get in the way? I encourage you to do away with any excuses and give conscious and consistent thought to getting mind and heart under control and in sync.

Encouraging Words: Matthew 14:28-31

WHAT, WHEN, AND
WHY DOES IT HAPPEN?

T he aging process seems almost cruel, totally out of alignment with what God desires for His children.

Pure innocence ultimately lost.

Pure innocence morphing into a slow progression of jaded and twisted thoughts and behaviors of varied degrees and styles.

How He must grieve—and yet He knows that this is how it will be, must be.

He gives us life, and He takes it, and He knows the in-between, all of it.

Oh, the things we are capable of, and do, in that in-between time of our own, from our time of pure innocence to when we breathe our last.

The change.

What, when, and why does it happen?

About Me: I had the pleasure recently of seeing something that grabbed my heart. In fact, it struck me to such a degree that I parked the car and watched for fifteen minutes. It was summer, and school was over for the summer season. But there was a program utilizing the school for kids to have a place to go and do things. At the time I was observing, it was playground time. In the enormous yard among all the playground equipment and play areas were approximately 150 young kids, all probably in the six-to ten-year-old bracket. The group was comprised of several ethnic groups. *And it seemed they were all happy (actually, gleeful), content, peaceful, polite, kind, and in more than a few cases, very loving.*

I saw absolutely no disharmony among them. They were all just being kids, happy kids at play. Some were holding hands, some had their arms around others, all of them were smiling. It was beautiful. It was wonderous. It gave me hope that perhaps someday there will be no cultural or racial boundaries, because I saw none in those moments. Witnessing the beauty of innocence, that day took me back many years to the time in my life when I was just like those kids. It was a time when the only boundaries to kids' innocence were the fences of the schoolyard and the amount of time left to play in it.

As I left the playground scene, my adult mind kicked in. My thoughts went from a deep sense of joy and hope over what I had just witnessed to shame and sadness over what I witnessed about my own life. It was abundantly clear. Over time, I had morphed from little Joey on a similar playground with similar kids surrounding me to teen Joe, and on to adult Joe, one full of biases, prejudices, agendas, motives, suspicions, lies, false love, etc. I was no longer innocent. I had changed. What happened? When did it happen? Why did it happen? Did it really have to happen? What might my adult life have been like had it not happened?

Then I thought of those kids again. Will loss of innocence happen to them? What will cause it? When will it happen? Why will it happen? What will their future lives be like because of it?

The answers to all the above were, I felt, succinctly delved into by something a learned friend of mine, author Jason Kanz, posted on social media just a few days following my observations at the playground and my ensuing thoughts. He has allowed me to share his thoughts:

> *Too much Christian parenting, it seems to me, is driven by fear. We seek to protect our children from the evil "out there," teaching them to be afraid of "the world" filled with sex, drugs, evolution, and the liberal media.*

> *How might our children come to understand the faith differently if they saw their parents utterly enamored by the surpassing beauty of Christ? I don't want my kids to be afraid of the world; I want them to fall in love with Jesus, who is the embodiment of love.*

Five small words: *fall in love with Jesus*. My own age of pure innocence is long gone. I'm quite far into that in-between time of my life, and I appreciate how all of those traits of adult Joe have changed for the better because of my love for Jesus (which came late in life) and because of the grace that came with the acceptance of His love. I also concluded that the answers to those questions I asked of myself really don't matter any longer. Jesus has got me, just as He always had me, but I needed to *fall in love with Jesus* in order to be the me that I am now.

As for the kids on the playground, I pray for several things. I pray that their morph from pure innocence to older adult may not be as harsh as the journey I trod. I pray that their parents will model for them by falling in love with Jesus. I pray that the transition from innocents to adults won't be too harsh on them, and that they will fall in love with Jesus on their own.

How special it would be if the what, when, and why questions would never have to apply to those kids.

What About You? If you have children, where do you see yourself as a parent? Do you think about your influence on your child's transition from innocence to adulthood? Putting Jesus as the center point of your family provides the necessary strengths for healthy parents building into healthy kids.

Encouraging Words: Luke 18:15-17

THE PERFECT MARRIAGE

A great marriage is not when the "perfect couple" comes together.
It is when an imperfect couple learns to enjoy their differences.
~ David Meurer[5]

Thoughts about a perfect marriage: The perfect marriage is the one between Christ and His church. Realistically, as humans, despite our best intentions, we cannot, and will not, have perfect marriages.

About Me: Mine is not.

What About You? If you are married, can you say yours is? If you are thinking marriage someday, how would you like yours to be?

Truth: There are great marriages. There are good marriages. There are bad marriages. And there are marriages in-between each of those. But there is no such thing as the perfect marriage. It would take the union of two perfect people to have the perfect marriage. Folks, none of us qualify to be those perfect people. Not now. Not ever. But maybe the following perspectives will provide insights for building into your marriage.

Love is a commitment that will be tested in the most vulnerable areas of spirituality, a commitment that will force you to make some very difficult choices. It is a commitment that demands that you deal with your lust, your greed, your pride, your power, your desire to control, your temper, your patience, and every area of temptation that the Bible clearly talks about. It demands the quality of commitment that Jesus demonstrates in His relationship with us. ~ Ravi Zacharias[6]

When two people are under the influence of the most violent, most insane, most delusive, and most transient of passions, they are required to swear that they will remain in that excited, abnormal, and exhausting condition continuously until death do them part. ~ George Bernard Shaw[7]

There are a few guidelines I know to be true about love and marriage: if you don't respect the other person, you're gonna have a lot of trouble. If you don't know how to compromise, you're gonna have a lot of trouble. If you can't talk openly about what goes on between you, you're gonna have a lot of trouble. And if you don't have a common set of values in life, you're gonna have a lot of trouble. Your values must be alike. ~ Morrie Schwartz[8]

This is not to disparage the thought of a good marital relationship at all. It is simply to set aside some illusions that folks sometime carry about the matter. The journey from "I do" through "happily ever after" is just that—a journey, and it is not unlike our personal journey through life. The whole thing of marriage is a constant learning process, a constant growth process, and, ideally, a constant spiritual process if it is Christ-centered. Marriage is of God's design, and He will always provide what we need to get through troubling times. If husband and wife mutually believe that, it's the basis for being blessed with a great marriage—something to which we can all aspire.

A CHALLENGE TO NORMAL

Imagine how hard it is to change yourself.
Then you'll understand what little chance you have
trying to change others.
~ Jacob M. Braude[9]

Normal. Is there such a thing? If so, what exactly is it? Normal for one person may not necessarily be normal for another. After all, "normal" as seen through the eye of the beholder is filtered through the lenses of society, our experiences, our baggage, and our belief systems. Thus, the question arises: Can what was once considered normal now be abnormal, and vice-versa? And once that question is answered, can we then change our concept of normal?

Relationships often suffer because of the varied concepts of what is or isn't normal within that relationship. Overcoming a roadblock to an otherwise healthy relationship may not be as easy as we would wish. If damage is already evident, it takes work and dedicated effort to get past that roadblock of lack of trust, lost or diminished sense of love, reduced caring, etc.

About Me: (Future subjects in this book have much shorter About Me's. Thanks for bearing with me on the length of this one.) I'm sharing the subject of "A Challenge to Normal" because of my marriage, all forty-plus years of it. Here's the deal. In the course of those forty-plus years, many of the early hopes, dreams, wishes, and even some expectations of the two of us either never occurred or simply got lost in the shuffle of growing older, growing a family, and doing life with all its ups and downs. As time accrued and older age set in, I found myself starting to dwell on those realities and found myself looking at, and seizing upon, more of the negatives than the positives about the marriage. I bought into thinking that present circumstances would be the forever norm. I found myself reflecting on what that process would, could, and did yield within me: unhappiness, boredom, failure, shame, a diminished sense of self-worth, and a world of wishful thinking based on what-ifs, what-could-have-beens, what-should-have-beens, and a whole lot of if-onlys. It was ugly thinking that I felt was normal.

Added to this was the fact that the marriage is what my faith teaching calls "unevenly yoked." When we married, neither of us was a believer. That has changed. I am now an active Christ-follower, attending an evangelical church, and my wife retains her beliefs in the denomination she's embraced since childhood, though she does not participate actively in the practices of that denomination. We are seemingly not opposed to what and how the other is, but the differences are evident in the ways we each act, communicate, think, and grasp certain life situations. It is not an active sore spot for either of us, but it is an underlying factor in how we view and do life individually and together. There is often an uncomfortable undercurrent felt by each of us.

Over the past several months while writing my thoughts for this book, my sense of what's normal has been challenged—thankfully. God evidently doesn't agree that what I was feeling was normal, and through several means, He's applied His corrective 2x4 to my head and heart about this marriage. He ever so gently reminded me that not only am I a child of God, *but so is my wife.* That correction convicted me that indeed I wasn't treating my wife, or thinking of her, in a godly manner.

Regardless of the circumstances, it has not been a bad marriage. But it has not been all that it could be, simply because I allowed myself to fall into the trap of what I (emphasis on the "I") deemed *should* be "normal." I at long last bought into the fact that change was needed, and that change had to start not with my wife, but with me. After all, how much of the developed-over-time "normal" resulted from my way of thinking about the marriage relationship? How much of the burden rested on my shoulders? In what ways was I personally responsible for the negativity I was feeling, and how did that affect my wife's feelings and actions? If

I really wanted to be truthful with myself, those hard questions had an easy answer: I was responsible for all of it.

Fortunately, and rightly so, God laid upon my heart one of His glorious plans. No more just thinking about it. It was time for action. Positive action. Godly action. Interestingly, it has turned out to be selfish action as well as selfless action, which I will explain in a bit. It became incredibly clear to me that while not overtly tearing down the marriage (though covertly, definitely), I was doing precious little to build up the marriage because of my accepting it as normal.

How has that changed? What was God's plan that grabbed my heart? Instead of just praying about it, I strongly felt that it was time to swallow my pride, see my shortcomings, step out on faith, and do the right thing. Shove the negativity aside and focus on only the good.

How could I do that? Post-It notes came to the rescue! I felt that notes, as opposed to any direct verbal comments, would be more helpful. I felt that the act of writing each morning a short little note with something about my wife that had put a smile on my heart and lips from the past day would be something that she could find and that would provide an element of surprise and, hopefully, an element of expectation. I felt that the act of writing notes for her to find would be a much less forced and a more thoughtful and deliberate means of saying something good. It also seemed better than something verbal that could possibly sound insincere at this early stage of me changing myself.

So, each morning, there is now a note on her teapot, the place she first goes to when she wakes up in the morning. The notes may be silly, corny, light-hearted, or deep, but they are always truthful and from the heart. There are no strings attached to this effort. I have no expectations. I don't ask if she has read them, nor will I. That's her business, not mine. All I know is that this is not a lose-lose effort, which it would be should I stop writing the notes. It is, therefore, either a lose-win or a win-win effort. Lose-win if she pays no attention to the notes, but I keep writing them. Win-win if she is happy about getting notes as I keep writing them. Even though my wife hasn't talked about the notes, it is quite evident that our "normal" demeanor has changed toward each other since the notes started. I must think it is a win-win.

And what I do know for certain is about the selfish part I alluded to earlier. *This has been good for me.* I feel built up because I am looking for, becoming aware of, and seeing firsthand the positive things about my wife and about our relationship that I have for so long neglected. I am much happier not dwelling on what I considered the negative things. Somehow, those things just don't seem all that important or all that negative anymore. Above all, I am secure in the fact that I am doing this husband thing in a godly way.

What About You Marrieds (and something to think about for the future for those of you in relationship)? Are you satisfied with your marriage? Can you accept the reality that marriage maybe is not what you had envisioned it to be, but rather, it is the coming together of two different people with different backgrounds, baggage, beliefs, and expectations? Can you accept that, regardless of those differences, each partner can and should conduct themselves in a godly manner, even if those manners vary somewhat? Can you accept that marriage is not 50-50, but rather 110-110 and that its success is predicated on what you put into it rather than what you take from it? With Christ as the center of your marriage, you will learn to appreciate each other, and sometimes even laugh together at your differences.

Encouraging Words: 1 Corinthians 13:4-7; Ephesians 5:31-32; Colossians 3:12-15

*You might be thinking, "I'm not perfect, I've made mistakes,
I mess up constantly, and I seem to be going the wrong way."
Remember, it's the "layers" in life that create the perfection.
Don't view your life as "mistakes"; view them as Da Vinci's layers,
and God is using your mistakes to help create a masterpiece with you.*
~ Trent Shelton[10]

WALLS

These walls are funny.
First you hate them, then you get used to them.
Enough time passes, you get so you depend on them.
That's institutionalized.
~ Ellis Boyd 'Red' Redding (Morgan Freeman),
The Shawshank Redemption[11]

Aren't we all somewhat institutionalized? In *The Shawshank Redemption* movie, the character Red was behind prison walls. Many of us are also behind walls, in a prison of another type. Our prison walls are the walls that, like Red's, keep us from being free. Free in Christ, and free in our relationships. They are the walls that we ourselves build. The walls that control our emotions, our responses, our reactions. The walls that affect how we live. And like Red said, we get used to them, then we depend on them, and eventually, they become our normal. Our walls may be constructed of such things as:

- Fear—fear of other's reactions toward us, fear of something new, fear of our inadequacies, etc.
- Shame—the shame we carry over past behavior(s), shame about something that happened to us in the past, shame about events over which we had no control, etc.
- False selves—false things that we haven't released, faced, or recognized as lies about us. False selves are the tools of Satan's workshop within our hearts and minds that stand in the way of us being all that we can be and are designed to be by God. They are negative things we are convinced of about ourselves,

and are most often expressed in our minds or to others using expressions similar to these:

- o I am not _____ because_____.
- o I can't because_____.
- o I will never be_____ because_____.
- o I am a bad person because_____.

These walls, which, over time, become our normal, are often why we become silent, closed off to others, distant, the sarcastic one, the clown, the spender, the fearful one, etc., or any combination.

Until the time comes in our lives when we face our self-inflicted walls and break out of the self-imposed prison, we will never fully appreciate full freedom, a freedom that comes from transparency, from meaningful relationships with others, and from an abiding relationship with Christ. We break free of our prison by casting those walls into the river of Grace, which has been given to us through Christ's death on the cross. At that point, we are no longer institutionalized, and we are free to create our new normal—in Him.

About Me: For a somewhat long while, I thought that I was in good shape spiritually, that I was okay. That is until I attended a Men at The Cross™ retreat (https://crossministrygroup.org/). Little did I know that some events that happened over six decades ago had shaped my thinking and clouded my heart to the degree which they had. As a result of those events, my "normal" was a deep-seated distrust of getting close to people and a deeply rooted feeling that at my core, I was a bad person. I thought I had a good relationship with Christ, but I was able to see that I lacked a full and complete understanding and appreciation of what true grace was all about. Only after deep soul-searching was I able to tearfully and emotionally break through those prison walls of my heart and mind that were keeping me from being truly free. I now know with absolute certainty that I am a free man. I matter to God. I am a child of God. And I am a godly man.

What About You? Do you dare look within yourself to discover what may be standing in the way of your having a closer relationship with Christ? Have you ever thought that you are being held prisoner by your thoughts, past hurts, shames, actions, or false selves? Have you considered that it is when you are in your self-imposed prison that the enemy is most happy? Have you ever tired of your normal, knowing that it wasn't really all that normal? What can, or will, you do about breaking free? Freedom is readily available to all who desire it and are willing to fight for it.

Encouraging Words: 2 Corinthians 5:17; Romans 12:2; Ephesians 5:8

Get busy living or get busy dying.
~ Andy Dufresne (Tim Robbins), *The Shawshank Redemption*[12]

DAVID AND GOLIATH

In life we all go through trials and tribulations.
So now tell me, will you pass, or will you make a mess?
~ Jonathan Anthony Burkett[13]

No, this isn't a re-hash of the Bible story of David and Goliath. This is about us, each of us. In many respects, we are just like the David and Goliath of that story. We each do life in many ways and styles. Some are at peace with ourselves, others not. Some struggle, others don't. Some feel lost, many don't. Just as with David and Goliath, our differences are as varied as our weights, heights, ages, and ethnicity. We are all individually different, and yet we are all so starkly similar. Ah, the beauty of God's creation—man.

And therein lies the key! Are we not all created by God? And that same God, because He created us, surely must have a plan for *each* of us. Therein lies both the beauty and the mystery of this thing called life, especially for those who believe in a creator God. We don't know the full extent of God's plan for our life, so how do we handle that? We should put our full trust in Him and follow His leadings. Often, however, we may not like and/or understand those leadings, and we may not want to follow them. Sometimes we may find ourselves in very troubled waters or black holes of despair. We may experience grief or pain that seems too much to bear. We may dig holes for ourselves that seem bottomless and hopeless. Our lives are seldom, if ever, picture-perfect, carefree lives of wondrous bliss, joy, peace, calm, and happiness.

Isn't it possible (and I believe it to be so) that part of God's plan is to place Goliaths in our paths so that we're forced to find the David within us? What better way is there to discover, while learning to trust and lean on God, that there is a David within us, a David that can beat any Goliath?

About Me: I walked through much of my life as a scoffer, one who had multiple addictions. Religion was for Bible thumpers. It was not until I was well into recovery that I discovered there was something much bigger (and better!) than myself, and that realization led to my becoming a believer. God showed that the David within me could beat those Goliaths. Other Goliaths that have reared their ugly heads on this continuing walk through life have also brought out the David within, and I know, just know, that each one is a part of God's plan for wherever He intends to take me. My only obligation is to keep trusting Him.

What About You? Could it help you to look at your shortcomings, behaviors, black holes, or problems as your Goliaths? Can you believe that there is a David within you, and that God wants your David to come alive and beat the Goliath? Do you trust God enough with your life that you allow Him to reveal His plan for you through your David and Goliath story? Each of us has a David and Goliath story somewhere within us that we can use for our own personal encouragement.

Encouraging Words: 1 Samuel 17:45; Proverbs 3:5; Jeremiah 29:11; Psalm 28:7

I AM

I am human.
I am imperfect.
I am incapable of being perfect.
I am always short of the glory of God.
I am a sinner.
I am a repentant sinner.
I am convinced that Christ died for my sin.
I am a believer.
I am a receiver of God's grace.
I am free.
I am a child of God.

About Me: I am, and I thank God I am.

What About You? How would you complete your statements of reality that begin "I am"? Trust me, no matter what or how many you list as your shortcomings, you can always end with *I am a child of God.*

Encouraging Words: John 14:6

SOCIAL INJUSTICE

Until the great mass of the people shall be filled
with the sense of responsibility for each other's welfare,
social justice can never be attained.
~ Helen Keller[14]

I have come to abhor use of the term "social justice" for several reasons:

- It has become toxic terminology and is highly politicized.
- It is used in conjunction with polarizing issues that are averse to peace and harmony within our culture.
- It is rarely compatible with the Bible's teaching of true justice.

All high-profile social justice groups have at least one core cause they stand for: same-sex marriage, abortion, affirmative action for women and select minorities, redistribution of legitimately accrued wealth and power, etc. My assessment of social justice groups is that they have very specific and narrow agendas, and they are in the business of playing on people's minds and seducing them with platitudes of righteousness while at the same time eschewing false passion and self-centered dislike for those who don't agree with them. The groups easily become divisive in nature, all under the banner of social justice. And the groups become harbingers of a strong feel-good mentality because of those who buy into and participate in their philosophies. Many keyboard warriors are born because of what they define as social justice.

Am I wrong in thinking that folks who buy into those movements and their public displays are often nothing more than pretenders? They feel good because they are a face in a mob (or a face covered up), they hold up an obnoxious sign, they wear embarrassing articles of clothing (or minimal clothing!), and yell themselves hoarse, often with profanities and inciteful invectives. In the supposed security of their like-minded cohorts, these pretenders say things and do things they would seldom say at the dinner table or do in the company of many of their rational friends. They go through the motions because they have been swayed by the hype and the planned process of gathering for the purpose of furthering an agenda or philosophy. The events are manufactured products, often misleading, and seldom without any substantive proposed solutions. Sadly, some social justice events are directed toward specific people for the positions they hold, and the mob can easily become vile, violent, raw, and ugly. In some instances, nothing is off limits. I find these attitudes and behaviors more specific to social *injustice* than resembling anything akin to social justice. And I find it extremely sad.

So, how is real social justice defined?

- It's when <u>you as an individual</u> treat all people equally, without regard for race, class, or creed.
- It's when <u>you as an individual</u> see an injustice and you step forward, without any agenda, to aid the victim.
- It's when <u>you as an individual</u> see something bad happening and you step up to confront it, even if there is the risk of personal condemnation.
- It's when <u>you</u> humbly act on what your heart and the Holy Spirit are prompting you to do, not with fear, but with confidence because you know it is the right thing to do.
- It's when <u>you</u> consistently treat *all* people with the same love you expect from others.
- It's when <u>your</u> actions, your utterances, and your public displays are all in sync with Christ's teachings.
- It's when all the above is <u>not</u> a one-time or occasional thing, but a lifestyle.

Real social justice is a one-on-one, one-person-at-a-time thing. It's you, becoming Jesus with today's skin on. It's you, being His light in a world of many who are less fortunate than you. It's you, countering all the negatives seen with social injustice. It's you, bearing (and baring) your responsibility as a Christ-follower.

Encouraging Words: Zechariah 7:9-10; Micah 6:8; Proverbs 31:8-9; Matthew 7:12; Matthew 19:21; Genesis 23:2

DEAR PORN DADDY

The truly scary thing about undiscovered lies is that
they have a greater capacity to diminish us than exposed ones.
They erode our strength, our self-esteem, our very foundation.
~ Cheryl Hughs[15]

The following is an unedited letter sent by a married woman to her father. It was posted on a parenting blog** and made anonymous due to the subject matter. It must have taken a lot of guts for the woman to write the letter and send it to her father. As you read, imagine the negative impact the father had on his daughter's young life to prompt writing this letter after such a length of time. And one must wonder what the father's reaction was when he read it.

Dear Dad:

I want to let you know first of all that I love you and I forgive you for what this has done to my life. You may think that this affects only you, or even your and mom's relationship. But it has had a profound impact on me and all of my siblings as well.

I found your porn on the computer somewhere around the age of 12 or so, just when I was becoming a young woman. First of all, it seemed very hypocritical to me that you were trying to teach me the value of what to let into my mind in terms of movies and music, yet here you were entertaining your mind with this junk on a regular basis. Your talks to me about being careful with what I watched meant virtually nothing.

Because of pornography, I was aware that mom was not the only woman you were looking at. I became acutely aware of your wandering eyes when we were out and about. This taught me that all men have a wandering eye and can't be trusted. I learned to distrust and even dislike men for the way they perceive women in this way.

As far as modesty goes, you tried to talk to me about how my dress affects those around me and how I should value myself for what I am on the inside. Your actions, however, told me that I would only ever truly be beautiful and accepted if I looked like the women on magazine covers or in porn. Your talks with me meant nothing and, in fact, just made me angry.

As I grew older, I only had this message reinforced by the culture we live in... that beauty is something that can only be achieved if you look like 'them.' I also learned to trust you less and less as what you told me didn't line up with what you did. I wondered more and more if I would ever find a man who would accept me and love me for me and not just a pretty face.

When I had friends over, I wondered how you perceived them. Did you see them as my friends, or did you see them as a pretty face in one of your fantasies? No girl should ever have to wonder that about the man who is supposed to be protecting her and the other women in his life.

I did meet a man. One of the first things I asked him about was his struggle with pornography, and I'm thankful to God that it is something that hasn't had a grip on his life. We still have struggles because of the deep-rooted distrust in my heart for men. Yes, your porn watching has affected my relationship with my husband years later.

If I could tell you one thing, it would be this: porn didn't just affect your life. It affected everyone around you in ways I don't think you could ever realize. It still affects me to this day as I realize the hold it has on our society. I dread the day when I have to talk to my sweet little boy about pornography and its far-reaching greedy hands, how pornography, like most sins, affects far more than just us.

Like I said, I have forgiven you. I am so thankful for the work that God has done in my life in this area. It is an area that I still struggle with from time to time, but I am thankful for God's grace and also my husband's. I do pray that you are past this and that the many men who struggle with this will have their eyes opened.

Love,
Your Daughter

Of all the things we do in our lives, any interest we might have in pornography is probably our most closely held secret. Interestingly, it might not be the secret we think it is; those close to us are often more perceptive than we might imagine. At its root, if you cannot talk about pornography, it owns you.

Recent studies vary, but there is agreement that between 60 percent and 70 percent of men who describe themselves as Christians view pornography (mostly on internet) regularly. The statistics are about half that for women. The statistics include pastors, ministry leaders, and church employees. Even infrequent use of pornography is an addiction. Overcoming that addiction is every bit as difficult as any other addiction, and usually more difficult because of the secrecy involved and the social stigmas attached to it.

About Me: My own spiritual journey included addressing pornography addiction. What brought about the change? A deep and serious contemplation of what integrity means. Simply put, if pornography was a part of my life, I had *no* integrity. Help came in the form of two trusted Christian men who accepted the role of accountability partners after some difficult discussions. And on all my electronic devices, I installed a Christian-based internet accountability program (©Covenant Eyes), which alerted me, *and them*, of any attempted website visits into the darker areas. My walk with God has improved exponentially in quality and depth since I chose to live with real integrity.

What About You? Are you owned by pornography? What stops you from doing something about it? Take solace in the fact that there is surely someone who is willing to walk alongside you toward healing should you choose full integrity as a lifestyle. Know that you are capable of casting this addiction aside because God has given you the strength to do so.

Encouraging Words: Romans 1:29; Galatians 5:29; 1 Corinthians 6:18
**shared by permission of the blog author

LEFTOVERS

Two men met and started to talk one day. One man introduced himself as Bob. The other never formally introduced himself. He was quiet, seemed interested, and was amazingly comfortable to be with. Bob, quite the extrovert and one who always enjoyed meeting new people, had no problem feeling safe in talking.

Bob, who always carried his lunch, explained at lunchtime that he had leftovers and that he always enjoyed them. He opined as how leftovers always seemed to taste better the next day. And he was happy that his wife always made certain that there were some that he could warm up for his lunch on cold days at work. Bob noticed that the quiet one didn't have lunch and just seemed to be hanging out.

Eventually, the conversation shifted, and the quiet one asked Bob if he went to church, and if he did, could he share a little bit about it. Bob shared that he and his family did go to church, though not as regularly as they probably could. He explained that he and the family liked to take care of matters such as yard work, shopping, car care, etc. on Saturdays, which left only Sunday to do fun stuff. Bob said that he and his wife liked to golf together, so in good weather, they packed in as much of that as they could on Sundays, the only convenient day to do so. And, Bob added, Sundays were always good days to do something that his wife enjoyed, like going to garage sales. Almost as an afterthought, he said that Sundays were also busy days for the kids' traveling team activities, which also limited their time for church. The quiet one asked Bob if he supported his church in any way. Bob got a little upset with that question and defensively responded, "Of course we do. We're Christians; we're supposed to do that."

The quiet one then asked what Bob did for a living. Bob really enjoyed talking about himself and so was not hesitant to answer. He told of how he had worked his way up to an executive level in his company and had finally reached the point in life where his financial security was not nearly the worry it had been in earlier years. He went on to brag about his wife being a real wizard with the household finances and how because of that they had enough in savings for his wife to live for several years in the comfort they were used to should anything happen to him. He took joy in the fact that they could afford good cars, had money in the bank for the kids' education, and could go out to eat whenever they wanted to.

The quiet one then asked Bob how he felt about the poor and impoverished in their area. Bob lit up with obvious pride. "You know," he said, "Jenny and I have a real soft spot for those people. Maybe two or three times a year, we go to the shelter and serve meals. We always take our old clothes to Goodwill, and we make it a point to donate occasionally to some of the drives for the poor and homeless. It's our duty as Christians, you know."

The quiet one pondered a minute on what he had heard and then asked a question that caught Bob by surprise: "You seem to like to share that you are a Christian. Do you get many opportunities to share your faith with others?"

Bob thought for a minute. "Actually, I don't do that. That is the minister's job. Besides, I do not know how or know enough to talk to anyone about that Jesus stuff. I mean, it's good and all to do that, but that's for other people to do."

Both men sat quietly for a minute. Bob, to break the silence, turned to the quiet one and asked, "I've got plenty of leftovers here. I would be glad to share them with you because I noticed that you're not eating. Would you like some?"

The quiet one looked at him sadly and replied, "No, I don't like leftovers. In fact, I hate them."

Bob was baffled by that answer. Then it dawned on him that he had never asked the quiet one his name. "By the way," he asked, "what's your name?"

The quiet one answered, "God. And all you give me is your leftovers."

Encouraging Words: Hosea 13:6; Malachi 1:8; Genesis 4:4-5; Luke 9:25; James 2:17

Even though you may want to move forward in your life,
you may have one foot on the brakes.
In order to be free, we must learn how to let go.
Release the hurt. Release the fear.
Refuse to entertain your old pain.
The energy it takes to hang onto the past
is holding you back from a new life.
What is it you would let go of today?
~ Mary Manin[16] Morrissey

ONE OF "THOSE" MOMENTS

They do not happen often. That is probably because we are too into the moment (or ourselves) to pick up on them. Or we're too busy, our minds are racing, or maybe we're simply not tuned in. But when we get one of "those" moments, we know it because it comes at us like a lightning bolt.

About Me: One of "those" moments came at me recently as I was driving to work, and like many of "those" moments, it came out of the blue. There was no catalytic reason, no logical or precipitating reason; it just popped into my head. It affected my heart (as "those" moments tend to do), and it had a major positive impact on me for the rest of the day.

My moment came when I realized that my outlook on life is vastly different now that I am a committed believer in Jesus Christ. I do not live like I used to, and I know just how awesomely blessed I am. My moment felt like a huge, warm, fuzzy comfort coat was wrapped around me; and as the day progressed, it stayed on me. It was a normal day in all other aspects, but that moment made it truly special. Wouldn't it be awesome if we were capable as humans of living "those" moments 24/7/365?

What About You? Maybe you're not a Christ-follower, but do you have "those" moments from time to time? Do you cherish them as specials? Do you find yourself wishing it would happen more often? Just what is it that makes them happen to us? It's "those" moments that often remind us that we can be in tune with all that God wants us to be.

Encouraging Words: Isaiah 43:2; Romans 15:13; Deuteronomy 28:1-68

How many times have you noticed
that it's the little quiet moments in the midst of life
that seem to give the rest extra-special meaning?
~ Fred Rogers[17]

A MERE BREATH AWAY

Breathe. Let go.
And remind yourself that this very moment
is the only one you know you have for sure.
~ Oprah Winfrey[18]

According to researchers, the average adult breathes between 17,280 and 23,040 breaths a day, and that is at rest. If we seriously want to contemplate our vulnerability and fragility, we need only consider how utterly and completely dependent we are on *every single breath* we take. We certainly do not consciously make breaths. Nor can we earn them. And, obviously, we absolutely cannot live without them. Each breath is much, much more than just a mere intake and release of air. But aren't we inclined to take each breath as just an automatic body function or a natural reflex? What if, per chance, suddenly, our next breath was not forthcoming? Without question, we would care about absolutely nothing else, and automatic panic would most likely set in.

Do we ever consider what a true gift each breath is? When God exhaled His own breath of life into Adam, Adam became a living being. That chain has <u>never</u> since been broken. We have all received the breath of life from that same God. Each breath we take is God's gift of grace, His living breath in us. Though every circumstance of our life hinges upon each of those ultimately millions of accumulated breaths we never seem to notice, we rarely think of them as indispensable or irreplaceable, do we?

God is as near to us as the last breath we have taken, most likely one we never even thought about. How might we be, as His people, if we were acutely aware of each breath and recognized it as not only a gift, but a priceless treasure? And what impact would we have on others if, through that recognition, we knew in our hearts that each exhalation was worthy of full gratitude for such a treasure from God? Perhaps there would be no time left for petty grievances, aggravation, anger, sadness, and, yes, sin. Godliness and holiness are but a mere breath away.

About Me: A simple thought about breathing graphically afforded me the opportunity to see how much I take for granted, how thankless I can be, and how worldly my mind can focus. Realizing those things pushed the next question to myself: How godly are my attitudes/reactions?

What About You? How much do you take for granted? How appreciative are you of *all* the gifts God has given you, even one as consciously unconscious as breathing? The significance of all that our bodies do completely on their own is wonderful evidence of God's awesome ways.

Encouraging Words: Genesis 2:7; Job 34:14-15; 1 Corinthians 6:19-20

LESSONS FROM MATH

$$6 + 3 = 9$$
$$5 + 4 = 9$$
$$7 + 2 = 9$$
$$8 + 1 = 9$$
$$9 + 0 = 9$$

The way we do things isn't always the only way to do them. In fact, there are arguably very few things that must be done in only one way. Folks manage their money in different ways. We decorate our homes in our own stylish ways. We maintain and landscape our yards to our own tastes. A trip on the freeway will certainly reveal that some folks drive very differently than others. And the list goes on.

We also do church and nurture our spiritual selves differently. Sometimes, that becomes a bone of contention as some people either secretly or openly become judgmental if another does not do things the way they do. Because we are humans, because we are broken (whether we accept that or not, or if we are yet unaware of it), and because God gave each of us the freedom to make choices (good ones or bad ones), we may do things differently than others.

So, what does the lesson from math tell us? We need to understand and appreciate that there are multiple ways of getting to a same end, and we should respect other people's ways of thinking in achieving that end. As it relates to spiritual growth, we must certainly respect and encourage a person's efforts rather than being judgmental or leaning on them to do it "our way." We must be patient with them, just as we must be willing to walk alongside them on their journey as they sort things out. God, through the Holy Spirit, is the one doing the work in their hearts, just as He did in ours. Our example may provide them more than anything we may say.

If they veer off track in their efforts for sound spiritual growth, we would be wise to remember our own journey. How steady was ours? Was it always a smooth progression of growth, or were there fits and starts? Was everything always clear when falling into place, or did we have to sort things out as we experienced setbacks? Were we more motivated in our search by the kind, loving, and patient encourager or by one who seized upon our mistakes and missteps in what seemed to be a judgmental manner?

About Me: Unless I am purposeful in my thinking, unless I look at myself hard, I can lean toward being judgmental about others as they begin their journey. It is an ugly way to think because it strips me of humility, something a seeker needs to experience in those around them. It makes me think that I am somehow better than they are, which I am not. We are both on the same journey, though in different places. I need to remember how I was nurtured by those around me during the early stages of my spiritual growth and how I responded as the learner. It was things such as openly practiced patience, love, kindness, and humility that created the atmosphere for me to want to seek more and learn more. Those around me respected where I was at and did not castigate me. And most of all, others were free in sharing with me their joy at seeing change taking place. They led me by walking alongside me through the journey, just as God continues to do each day.

What About You? To be completely honest with yourself, how judgmental are you of others? Is "it's my way or the highway" a part of your mindset? In terms of another's spiritual walk, do you grasp the simplicity and lack of detailed instructions in the suggested Scripture, and can you accept the importance of that? How do you share your joy as you watch someone near you embrace Christianity? Just as we acknowledge and appreciate our own differences, we should appreciate differences in others.

Encouraging Words: 1 Peter 5:1-5; Titus 2:6-8; Proverbs 2:7; Hebrews 5:12-14

Have a big enough heart to love unconditionally,
and a broad enough mind to embrace the
differences that make each of us unique.
~ D. B. Harrop[19]

I CAN'T

"I can't do this."
"I can't understand that."
"I can't kick this habit."
"I can't stop doing that."
"I can't believe that."
ad nauseum

Those two little words, "I can't," permeate our thoughts and spoken words much more than they should or, more importantly, must. They are a vivid reflection of our inner selves, of our belief structure. That is sad, because when we utter those words, or think them, we are abdicating our willingness to rely on and trust the very God who made us. We are telling ourselves that we are the ones in control and that we cannot do it, whatever "it" is.

By balking and insisting "we can't," we are also denying our Lord the opportunity to mold us into the people we can be. We do that because deep down we believe that we know what is best for us and which paths *we* want to take in our life's journey. But isn't much of what we do centered around our perceived comfort levels? How do all those past bad decisions and choices we have made stack up next to a good, healthy comfort level?

What a wonderful world it could be if none of us ever again said "I can't."

About Me: I am convinced at this stage of my life that God is not concerned with, nor does He appreciate, my idea of a comfort level. I am quite sure that He's most concerned about the person I can be if I just trust Him and allow Him to do His work in and through me. That can only be accomplished when I stop saying or thinking "I can't" and start focusing on how I can do all things through Him.

What About You? Truthfully, have you ever thought for a minute that God led you astray or put you on the wrong path? Have you ever considered that perhaps *you* led yourself astray onto the wrong path, and if so, did you or can you own it? Consider leaning into a new leader—namely, God. In choosing God's help, we can all turn our "I can't" into "I can."

Encouraging Words: Ephesians 3:20

Embrace the unexpected.
It could be one of God's surprises!
~ unknown

WE'RE ALL BOTTLES

Nothing can disturb you unless you allow it to.
~ Roy T. Bennett[20]

Let's say, for the sake of argument, that we are all bottles. I'm a bottle. You're a bottle. We're all bottles—but which one? Inside those bottles are our emotions and our reactions. Just like a bottle of water or a bottle of soda, we get shook up sometimes. Circumstances and people can rattle us, and we react. It is part of life. It is going to happen.

What happens when you drop or shake a bottle of soda before opening it? It is going to spew with fizz and soda running all over the place when you open it. It is not pretty, and it leaves a sticky mess behind.

But...if you shake up a bottle of water, what happens when you open it? It is the same calm water as before it was shaken. No fizz. No mess.

My analogy: When we lose our inner peace and calm, becoming rattled and all shook up over circumstances or something someone did to us, isn't it better that we NOT be like the bottles of soda, but rather like the bottles of water?

About Me: "Create a crisis" could have been my nickname in my younger adult days (and in a few not-so-young adult days). Those around me knew all too well that I couldn't be happy unless I was shook up, worked up, or rattled by someone or some circumstance around me, and in my arrogance, I had to be parading that attitude to everyone around me. Chaos was the norm. Calm was the rarity. Only when I fully grasped that God's got my back no matter what stuff happens was I able to grab hold of and appreciate what a sense of inner peace and calm was. That is reliance—reliance on the fact that God knows what is happening, and reliance that whatever happens is an opportunity for me to lean into and learn more from Him. It helped me learn to release to Him those times that would previously have caused a reaction of crisis or chaos in me.

What About You? When life throws life at you, what's in your bottle? Soda or water? If it is soda, ask yourself if living fizzed up and ready to explode is what you want. If it is water, keep working diligently on reacting to difficult real-life situations with a peace and calmness that settles you and is evident to others. Believe me, that is most definitely what God genuinely wants for you. Believe me too—you are allowed the occasional fizz-up. Just take a deep breath and think water!

Encouraging Words: Philippians 4:6-7; Isaiah 41:10; Joshua 1:9; 2 Timothy 1:7

CRITICAL THINKERS

*I shiver, thinking how easy it is to be totally wrong about people
—to see one tiny part of them and confuse it for the whole, t
o see the cause and think it's the effect or vice versa.*
~ Lauren Oliver[21]

S ome folks are wired up such that their minds reach into depths my
mind seldom reaches. Their uncanny ability to process information
on the fly; effortlessly weed out fact from fiction; and come up with a
correct, wise, and godly bullet-proof response or solution amazes me.
These I define as "great" critical thinkers.

Now it took me a while to realize that I also can be a critical thinker,
but I realized my critical thinking is not the same as the ones above.
Maybe you share with me in a category where we would be more appro-
priately called "worldly" critical thinkers.

Here is what I realized about how my critical thinking works, and
it all happened in five short minutes. As I always do, I was walking the
dog one morning. It was early, and like most mornings, I was enjoying
the calm and tranquility of the walk—until I saw the truck, observed
the flowerboxes, and heard the car horn, each in close succession to the
other and each setting up opportunity for my kind of critical thinking.
The truck with its loud muffler did a poor imitation of a California stop
at the stop sign. (Apologies to Californians, but I think they understand
the critique.) The flowerboxes on the front windows of the neighbor's
house were empty, void of flowers, as they have been the past five years.
And as happens every day at 5:30 a.m., the same car sat out in front of
another neighbor's house, repeatedly blasting the horn for the person

who was to ride with them. And so, with my brand of critical thinking coming to the fore, I muttered some self-talk about the lousy driving and noise from the truck, about the laziness of the neighbor for having empty flowerboxes, and about the blaring horn and the inability of the person in the house to be ready for his ride each day. Truck, flowerboxes, and horn—all within five minutes and all stirring my annoyance.

But then as some critical, critical thinking kicked in, I laid into myself for being so reactive about those things that, a) I have no control over, and b) are really none of my business. In that moment, I realized the frequency of my type of critical thinking and what a waste of time and effort it is. I pondered how better that time could be if I used it to bask in the goodness of God instead and warmed myself with thoughts of the grace He has heaped upon me. Then it hit me. I bet Jesus would never fret about trucks, flowerboxes, or horns if He walked my neighborhood today. He would always be too busy doing His work. Then the question came: Why can't I do the same?

About Me: The above examples showed a flaw in my sense of godliness and holiness. I was able to see how, if I truly want to be a godly and holy man, there is no room for that kind of "worldly" critical thinking of making myself better than others, when in fact I am not.

What About You? Are you a critical thinker? Which type? Because most of our thoughts remain in our heads where others are unaware of them, does this give you free reign to be one of the "worldly" critical thinkers? How could you change your reactive thinking? Most of us, including you, reactively think less than we may give ourselves credit for. Lean into that as a blessing, and then give yourself the freedom to change the thinking that you are uncomfortable with.

Encouraging Words: Proverbs 14:15; 1 John 4:2; 1 Thessalonians 5:22

PLAY THE ODDS

I am not sure what heaven will be like,
but I know that when we die and it comes time for God to judge us,
He will not ask, "How many good things have you done in your life?"
Rather he will ask, "How much love did you put into what you did?"
~ Mother Teresa[22]

Man suffers fatal heart attack on local golf course
Mother of four perishes in car accident on Rt. 142
High school football player tragically dies on the field

Headlines and news leads such as the above are not uncommon. Many other deaths we do not hear of unless we are family of or know the deceased through work, by association, etc. If those deaths were published as news articles, they might read something like this:

Husband dies during dinner from fatal heart attack
Wife passes away during surgery
Friend dies from cancer

The inevitability of death is something we all acknowledge. We know that death is something we all will ultimately experience. But how many of us honestly think of our own death in any way other than acknowledging that it is something we can't escape and it's something that lies somewhere in the future, hopefully the far future? Do we ever seriously consider that it could occur in as short a time as our next breath? Do we ever think that it can be as immediate and stark as turning off the light switch which plunges the well-lit room into total darkness instantly? Some of us glimpse that thought occasionally, but we drop it quickly because it is not a comfortable thought. The probability of one's own impending death isn't a pleasant thought for many of us.

In our reticence to embrace thoughts of our own death, we are essentially playing the odds. By not looking at the complete inevitability of it, which includes the fact that it could occur with our next natural breath, or the next intersection we cross while driving, or being a random victim in the right place at the wrong time, we're telling ourselves that we have plenty of time to get our spiritual house in order. Isn't that playing the odds, especially if our house is *not* in order?

Talking and thinking about our own deaths should not be maudlin, denied, or considered strange. And it is none of those when we have embraced Jesus Christ as our Savior and live as He would have us live.

About Me: I do not want to die yet, but I know it could happen before I put the period at the end of this sentence. And yet, I have the security that when I die, I will be with Jesus. I will not be there because some pastor or minister stood before my family and other attendees telling them I'm going to be with the Lord in heaven. I have heard that message at funerals where the best I could do was pray and I simply prayed that it was true. I believe what the Bible says about going to heaven, and I am doing my earthly best to live in such a way as to hear those words I want to hear, "Well done, My faithful son," at the end of my ride here on earth. I want to know I am ready for that next breath that may not come, that next intersection I may not safely get through, or for that time when I may be in the right place at the wrong time. I don't like to play the odds. It is not Jesus's way. He didn't play the odds.

What About You? Do you play the odds? Do you really think you have plenty of time to take care of business before you die? What is better, a life of same old-same old, or a life of being prepared and knowing you are ready when your time comes? Again, do you play the odds? The stakes, His Kingdom, are far too valuable to foolishly bet on.

Encouraging Words: Matthew 24:44; Matthew 25:13; Proverbs 20:4; John 14:6; Matthew 24:42; Luke 16:19-31

YOU ARE A PIECE OF WORK

The reason why so many are still troubled,
still seeking, still making so little forward progress is because
they haven't yet come to the end of themselves.
We're still trying to give orders and interfering with God's work within us.
~ A. W. Tozer[23]

I t is not uncommon to hear the term "You're a piece of work." It is one that is used in an assortment of different contexts. For example:

- It may be used as an expression of incredulity.
- It may be an expression of disgust.
- It might serve as an opinion that one is over-the-top crazy.

Like it or not, each of us is, in the final analysis, a piece of work. A very real piece of work. Indeed, we are all works in progress, and we will remain so until we depart this earth. My religious belief is that God starts a work in us before we are born, and His work continues in us throughout our lives. As you read this, He is still working in you and me, and He WILL finish that work. Of that, we can be certain. And it is only through the choices we make about how we conduct our lives that we discover how He will finish it.

About Me: I have been told more than a few times in my life, "You're a piece of work." I clearly remember the time the police chief said it to me. On a police force at the time, I had been summoned to the chief's office. Cops dread those calls. It turned out the chief wanted to see me because he had heard through the grapevine that I was applying for a position with the State Police. He wanted to know what was going on. After I explained myself (which, in retrospect, was quite lame and naive), he simply shook his head, looked at me, smiled, and said, "You know, Joe, you're a piece of work." I ultimately stayed with the local force and enjoyed a fantastic career there.

Later in life, during a discussion with my wife (okay, it was more than a discussion), I vividly remember her putting me down in a big way with the cutting remark, "You're a piece of work." At the time, she was right. I was being unreasonable.

Then there was the time when a group of us guys were horsing around, laughing, and being outlandishly silly. One of the guys laughed through his tears and yelled, "Joe, you're a real piece of work." That was during the time in my life when I was still frequently over-indulging in adult liquid refreshments and was prone to doing real stupid things.

These days, I rather enjoy the thought that perhaps God is smiling down at me, shaking His head, and saying to Himself, "I have a good thing going with that piece of work." God knows that I blow it sometimes, yet He continues to bless me and cover me with His grace.

Those of us who have embraced Christianity are aware of the wonderful work that God has done with us, in us, for us, and through us. We also know that there is a progression of His work that is not yet completed, and we hold dear to the fact that the best is yet to come. Our journey is His work, and it will only be completed at that time when He takes us to His home.

What About You? If you have not embraced it already, I encourage you to consider the fact that you are a piece of work—God's work. Can you, even if a non-believer, reflect on your past and see how God's hand has been all over your life? Are you willing to yield to His guidance as He continues to work in you in your present life? Will you embrace, with awe and excitement, where He is leading you? As you see evidence of God's hand on your life, see it as a blessing, one you want more of.

Encouraging Words: 1 Thessalonians 2:13; Ephesians 2:10; Philippians 2:13

To be a Christian means to forgive the inexcusable
because God has forgiven the inexcusable in you.
~ C. S. Lewis[24]

DUELING VOICES

I don't know how to answer.
I know what I think,
but words in the head are like underwater.
They are distorted.
~ Jeanette Winterson[25]

Dueling banjos or pianos are pleasing to hear. Dueling voices, not so much. The trouble is, we probably hear far more of the dueling voices than we do of either the banjos or pianos. And since we inherently possess a sinful nature, we may tend to listen to one over the other of those voices that reside in our head. That is when we find ourselves in a jam.

God's Voice	Satan's Voice
stills us	rushes us
leads us	pushes us
reassures us	frightens us
enlightens us	confuses us
comforts us	worries us
calms us	obsesses us
commends us	condemns us

God's voice builds us up and places us on the path toward righteousness. Satan's voice tears us down and leads us on a path toward self-reliance. Both voices know our weaknesses, but only one wants to strengthen those weaknesses. The other plays on those weaknesses to further weaken us.

God's voice is often that still, small voice we hear, but it is always right on time and *always* for our good and the furtherance of His plan for us. Unfortunately, Satan's voice is often the louder of the two and is *never* for our good or the furtherance of God's plan.

God is a God of love and order. If the voice we hear is not about love or order, then it's not from Him, and it means we're listening to the wrong one of those dueling voices.

About Me: One of my greatest weaknesses has been that of self-control. I want full control and have always found it difficult to let go and let God. Satan's voice has always played to that weakness, loudly and clearly. As a result, many of the choices and decisions I have made have not been God-honoring. One way I now strive to overcome that problem is to wait before reacting or responding to a situation or thought, allowing time for God's voice to calm me.

What About You? Do you sometimes find the thoughts about choices you must make conflicted? Is it possible that Satan is playing to your weaknesses at those times? Do you tend to make quick decisions, or do you take time to allow the dust to settle so that you can make informed decisions? Do you have a pattern of making decisions that aren't God honoring? How can you overcome that? Your good choices will define you as a godly person.

Encouraging Words: Matthew 11:28-30; Galatians 6:2; John 16:33; Psalm 145:14

I HAVE A LOT OF RESPONSIBILITIES

My words

~~Words of others~~

My behavior

~~Others' behavior~~

My efforts

~~Others' efforts~~

My decisions

~~Others' decisions~~

My actions

~~Others' actions~~

My mistakes

~~Others' mistakes~~

My choices

~~Others' choices~~

My beliefs

~~Others' beliefs~~

Just taking care of my own business

Make someone happy today and mind your own business.
~ Ann Landers[26]

EYES LIKE JESUS

What we do for ourselves dies with us.
What we do for others and the world remains and is immortal.
~ Albert Pike[27]

At times, I have wondered about Jesus's eyes when He was here on earth. It would be interesting to know if they were blue, green, or perhaps steel grey. I can only guess if they were widespread eyes or close. And while I know that at times in His life, they were likely sad, I wonder how Jesus's eyes were most of the time. Piercing, soft, sharp, fully focused? Were they cautious and wary, or perhaps steady and assured? The fact is, none of that matters, does it? None of it is important. I have come to realize that all we need to consider about Jesus's eyes are the things that He saw and, more importantly, *how He responded* when He saw those things.

- He saw the differences in people. But He saw them deeper than I often do. He saw their hearts first.
- He saw the weaknesses and faults in people. And He always saw opportunity for teaching and spiritual healing in them—something I often fail to do.
- He saw the differing status of people, yet He saw them all as equals. My biases and prejudices are not always held in check.
- He never failed to see pain and suffering, and His focus was on compassion and healing for everyone He came across. My self-absorption can detract from empathy for the plight of others.

- He saw homelessness, hunger, and hardship. And when he saw the need for provision, He provided. As for me, too often I look the other way and find a way to justify stinginess.
- He saw divisiveness, and He stressed the need for unity. How many times have I fed divisiveness instead of brokering unity? Too many.

About Me: Yes, I still have plenty of work to do because I do not have eyes like Jesus.

What About You? It's okay to give yourself credit when you respond to others in ways that Jesus might have. Remember, you can be the hands and feet of Him.

HAPPINESS

Many people lose the small joys in the hope for the big happiness.
~ Pearl S. Buck[28]

Happiness. It's defined as the state of being happy, a state of contentment or well-being. There are folks who always seem happy, often to the extreme (the Mr. or Mrs. Happy). And there are those at the opposite end of the spectrum who are never happy (the Debbie or Davy Downer). Most of us, however, are often somewhere in between. And many of us spend a lot of time and effort to find happiness, in good ways and in bad ways.

Surely, there is nothing wrong with being happy. We all desire it in our lives. But what if I said that happiness is overrated, or sometimes superficial? Would it rock your world if I said that there is often too much emphasis placed on being happy or trying to achieve happiness when what might be missing is the element of joy in one's life?

Frankly, I hold the belief that happiness is a rather worldly term. It is something we seek or try to gain or believe we can achieve, even though it may be at the expense of others. My point is that happiness is something people create or maybe play a role in when it occurs. Joy, on the other hand, as Christians recognize, is from the heart. It is the gift of contentment, which we know comes out of our relationship with Christ. It is through that relationship that we learn to be content with God's provision for us as we rely on Him to meet our needs according to His plan. We trust Him. We have faith.

About Me: As one who struggled with alcohol, drugs, sex, and irresponsibility, I took a lot of hard knocks before reaching the conclusion that there was no way I was *ever* fixing myself. I could fix lots of other things, but I alone could not fix me. Although I spent tons of money buying things and creating situations to try to make me happy, and I was happy a lot, it never lasted. More was always necessary to keep the happy bug fed. And deep down, I was never genuinely happy. I realized that much of what I thought could lead to lasting happiness was both superficial and fleeting. It took allowing God, acceptance of Jesus, and transparency in Christian community into my life before I was fixable. Joy came only when that empty spot in my heart, that spot that always yearned for "something," got filled with a love of the Lord and reliance on Him in my life.

What About You? Are there emotional parts of you that need to get fixed? Does your heart nudge you about those parts? If you are a Christian, how real and how committed is your walk of faith? Are you in community with others? Are you transparent in that community? If not, why not? Please know you can trust that God can and does fix His children with the intensely deep emotion of joy. He will never fail you.

Encouraging Words: Isaiah 41:10; Isaiah 53:5; Romans 12:1-2; Psalm 147:3; James 5:16

I DIDN'T

The function of prayer is not to influence God,
but rather to change the nature of the one who prays.
~ Soren Kierkegaard[29]

ABOUT ME:

I didn't die today or come down with any illness.
I didn't get fired or laid off from my job today.
I didn't come home to find that my wife had left me.
I didn't get into an accident or lose my way while driving today.
I didn't get injured today.
I didn't forget any important things today.
I didn't yell at, curse, or think bad things of anyone today.
I didn't forget to stop on the way home and pick up some things that I was asked to.
I didn't goof off at work today.
I didn't forget to try to think only nice things about others today.
I didn't lust or have lewd thoughts today.

Oh, yeah, there is one other—I didn't thank God for all my *didn'ts* today. I was too busy being proud of myself to focus on the fact that it is because He is ever-present and in control of my life that a lot of things did not happen.

When we pray, we often ignore the good things about ourselves, even if they are routine and possibly mundane. Those didn'ts listed for my day are some of the blessings we can all relate to as we daily go about living life, and yet we tend to ignore them. Aren't they equally as important as our prayers for that new job we are seeking, or a way out from some bad decisions we have made, or relief from an illness we may be struggling with? Our didn'ts are another reminder of the sovereignty of God and how His hand covers us, even when we are unaware or fail to give conscious thought to it. Often when we pray, we are so involved in trying to make our words sound right that we fail to share our joy in having some didn'ts.

What About You? How is your prayer life? Is it a good conversation with God, or does it sound more like a well-practiced speech? How thankful are you for the things (didn'ts or otherwise) that we assume are not all that important to acknowledge to God? Take a minute to look back on your day and acknowledge those times when God's hand was over your life in different ways and situations.

Encouraging Words: 1 Chronicles 29:11-12; Proverbs 19:21; Daniel 4:35

HERE I AM

Great moves of God are usually preceded by simple acts of obedience.
~ Stephen Furtick[30]

Three little words. Spoken by three biblical men of God. A powerful example for us. The words, while easy enough to annunciate, are at times difficult for us to say with real conviction and even harder to follow through on because we feel our faith is being stretched past the limits we're unaccustomed to. Those three words can sometimes cruelly expose our brokenness.

Abraham, Moses, and Samuel each uttered those three words with conviction and with follow-through. They had faith far greater than many of us in today's time. They trusted God at all costs. How many of us can truthfully say the same?

Those three little words for those three men meant two things:

- They were <u>readily</u> available.
- They were <u>totally</u> obedient.

For each man, their faith was stretched to a degree we might find extreme:

Abraham, called upon by God to offer his own son as a burnt offering, was on the verge of lighting the fire under his son when God intervened. How is that for being available and being fully obedient?

Moses, who had just come from forty years as a shepherd, took charge and led the rebellion of the Israelite slaves. That was an epic undertaking. Moses knew it would be no picnic in the park, but he did it.

Samuel, a biblical judge, and prophet, stepped way out on a limb and called the Lord's judgment on the lineage of priests in Israel. Talk about jumping into a fire!

If we were to investigate the full context of each of those examples, we could legitimately consider that each of those men had a nature quite separate from most of us. They were in relationship with the Lord and *completely* trusted Him. Because of that, they were self-disciplined to the degree that they could say those three little words, mean it, and follow through with what God wanted of them.

When the words "Here I am" are honestly and truthfully spoken, God carries out His plan by his own response of "Here I am."

About Me: When I finally acquiesce to what I know God wants me to do and utter those three words, it is normally after I have wrestled with Him and felt some unnecessary pain or discomfort. It is at those times, when the dust has settled, that I once again realize that I'm not in control, but God is. And it is in those times moments when I hear Him the loudest as He reminds me once more: "Here I am." Will I ever learn?

What About You? Do you hear God when He is calling? Are you ready for His call? How prepared are you to say without hesitation, "Here I am"? This is something that is fully God-honoring. If you are not accustomed to it, try taking baby steps as you tune in to Him, and then allow yourself to trust where He leads you. You may be amazed by what you find.

Encouraging Words: Genesis 22:1-14; Exodus 14; 1 Samuel 3:1-4:22

GREAT BIG COW

It is about the greatness of God,
not the significance of man.
God made man small and the universe big
to say something about himself.
~ John Piper[31]

For the past three years, I have been blown away by something I see every morning at work. I often stop simply to stare because I have been udderly—yes, udderly—amazed. Pun intended because this object of wonderment is a cow. Not just any cow, but a great big cow. An overwhelmingly huge cow. An oversized cow that hangs out with four other normal-sized cows at the farm next to where I work. The difference in size between the cows is stunning, mind-boggling. One just does not see cows of that extreme girth very often.

About Me: Stopping to stare at the great big cow one recent morning when a beautiful sunrise painted the sky as a backdrop, my thoughts moved to something else that is huge beyond description. That something is our God. Who but a great big God made that beautiful sunrise for me to see? Who but a great big God made that great big cow for me to see? Who but a great big God made this body that I inhabit, the one that breathes on its own, the one whose heart has pumped regularly and rhythmically for all these years? Who but a great big God made me and gave me life I all too often take for granted?

Yes, I thought, *that is one great big cow I'm looking at, but nowhere near as big as the great big God who created both it and me. That cow* and I have something in common. Neither of us is as big as our great big God, nor as timeless. He is forever; we're not. And He is the one who made us both.

What About You? Do you take your last breath and your next breath for granted, that they just happen? Do you let your thoughts drift to God, the source, the real source, of all you see, do, and are? Is God, in your mind, a great big God? Seeing God from that perspective gives us such a wonderful sense of how blessed we truly are, despite our circumstances. Hopefully, you are feeling the blessing.

Encouraging Words: Jeremiah 23:23-24; Psalm 90:2; Jeremiah 32:17; Psalm 139:14

LIFE IS LIKE A
CUP OF COFFEE

As believers, our reaction to crisis reveals our heart toward God.
~ Andrena Sawyer[32]

To many of us, a cup of coffee (or two or three) in the morning is what jump starts our day. Health matters aside, it is the gold standard of the get up/get moving/get going process many of us think we need as we begin our days. While some of us cannot imagine starting the day without coffee, others cannot imagine starting the day with it. It is a matter of personal choice. Likewise, life itself is a matter of many choices.

Imagine that you are holding that cup of coffee (yeah, for this segment, I'm just going to assume all you readers are coffee junkies) and someone bumps into you, causing the liquid to spill. Why did the coffee spill? It spilled because it was what was in your cup when you were bumped.

In life, we are that cup. When life happens, as it always does, and we get bumped, whatever is inside the "us" cup is going to spill out in some way. When we experience the little bumps, we are usually adept at taking it and faking it gracefully. However, when it is a hard bump, we often get rattled. When we get those hard bumps, will joy, gratefulness, peace, and humility spill out? Or do harsh words, bad reactions, anger, and bitterness pour forth? We have got to know how to handle what's in our cup because what spills out is an indication of how the heart acts as a lid on our emotional cup. When the heart-lid senses harsh or hateful responses to whatever the situation, it needs to stay on tightly to deter the negatives from pouring forth. But when it senses gratitude, joy, kindness, gentleness, forgiveness, affirming words, and unconditional love for others—not always easy—it is happy to get flipped off the cup in order to allow myriad goodness to spill out.

About Me: Perhaps one of the most difficult battles I have faced over the years is changing what spills out of my cup when life bumps me. I know how terrible and sinful my spillage can be. My spiritual journey has brought me to the point that when spillage happens and I feel my response will come out in an awfully bad way, I just can't let it pass. I am so grateful that I have learned to acknowledge that I just messed up and that I need to address it properly right then and there. I enjoy that little, but important, bit of progress.

What About You? When your cup spills, do you later find yourself lamenting your reaction? With spills, consider the effect what pours out will have on those around you. The more you practice, the better those spills to come will be.

Encouraging Words: Psalm 139:23

NAKEDNESS

Over the years you will go through seasons in which you have to learn
to love a person you didn't marry, who is something of a stranger.
You will have to make changes that you didn't want to make,
and so will your spouse. The journey may eventually take you into
a strong, tender, joyful marriage. But it is not because you married
the perfectly compatible person. That person doesn't exist.
~ Timothy Keller[33]

It is a reasonable assumption to say we've probably all seen our spouses naked. But have we seen what is under the skin, seen what is hiding inside, seen their raw inner nakedness? If we have not exposed ourselves fully to our marriage partner, can we expect anything more from them? If we are hiding our own inner self, how can we not expect the same from our spouse? How can we expect a deeply spiritual relationship without sharing our true, deep, and raw inner nakedness? Maybe the questions that follow are ones whose answers you have never sought from your spouse, let alone answered for yourself:

What are his or her dreams and hopes?
What is he or she deeply passionate about?
What does he or she feel is his or her life's purpose?
What breaks his or her heart?
What makes him or her cry?
What are his or her deepest hurts?
What brings him or her to silence?

What reaches deep inside him or her and draws out raw feelings
and emotion?
What causes him or her to simply beam with joy?
What does he or she consider broken about themselves?
What does he or she find difficult to share openly?
What is his or her biggest perceived (or real) failure?
What has he or she given up because he or she loves you?
More for you to think about:
What do you really know about his or her childhood?
What story about him or her are you not in?
What secrets does he or she carry about themselves that you now
know about?
What baggage that he or she is carrying don't you know about?
What could he or she talk about that you really desire to hear?

About Me: Through many years of marriage (forty-plus), I have begun
to think a lot about the depth of my spousal relationship. I have thought
about some of the lost dreams we held earlier on, the hopes that diminished, and the oomph of the marriage that eroded into a dwindling
sense of complacency. After all these years of marriage, I have come to
realize that my spouse and I know very precious little about each other's
raw nakedness. I also know that it does not have to be that way. In fact,
it would be a healthier relationship were it not. Further, I now realize
that being unevenly yoked (as my spouse and I are) is no excuse for not
having a healthier relationship. As a Christ-follower, my responsibility
is to model a godly life continually, patiently, and lovingly, one that fear-
lessly embraces transparency without judgment and one that is confident in the reality that hope is never lost. Most importantly, I must trust
in God's good timing for all results.

What About You? How naked is your marriage? Do you know the
answers to the suggested questions? Would you evade answering some
of those questions if asked of you? By putting God at the center of your
marriage, you can slowly, lovingly, and thoughtfully explore those questions together to discover the real (both of) you.

Encouraging Words: Ephesians 5:21-33

MAKE BETTER BETTER

*The world needs Christians
who don't tolerate the complacency of their lives.*
~ Francis Chan[34]

"That's good enough." "Well, I've done my best, I can't get it better than that."

Sound familiar? How often do we make those statements? Aren't they indicators of complacency? Doesn't complacency often lead to apathy? Isn't apathy one of the devil's hand tools?

Most folks I know are better people now than the people they were in earlier chapters of their lives. They got to their better standard by not being complacent, and certainly by not being apathetic, about themselves or their lives. When we encounter whatever is our stumbling block, it is a good sign that we know we don't want to fall into the trap of complacency and eventual apathy. I have been there and done that, and it was an ugly climb back to becoming my better person.

Our hope as rational people should always be to make better better. We should never be satisfied. Striving always to make better better, and living that out in our spiritual life, will extend into the physical, mental, emotional aspects of our lives. We <u>will</u> become people who make better better.

About Me: My rut was living a sinful, irresponsible life. A key component of my thinking during those times was "I can't be better than I am." I was resigned to be that person who I was at the time. It was only when I started to address my spiritual sickness that the other wounded areas of my life started to heal as well. I know this was not accomplished on my own. It was the work of the Holy Spirit within me and of others who did His earthly handiwork on me, thus causing my better to become better. By the way, it did not happen overnight. He had to put in a lot of overtime!

What About You? Do you settle for less than your absolute best when it comes to your spiritual life? You can rest assured that Jesus, our prime example of how to live, was never complacent, never apathetic. Take the necessary time to give thought to how you can move forward when those less-than attitudes present themselves in your life. You are definitely worth it.

Encouraging Words: Proverbs 1:32; Revelation 3:15-16; Hebrews 5:11-12

MASTERPIECE

The Bible does not say you are God's appliance;
it says you are His masterpiece.
Appliances get mass produced.
Masterpieces...handcrafted.
~ John Ortberg[35]

Insignificant. Insecure. Not good enough. Irrelevant. Undeserving. Imposter. Pretender.

Those are some of the words we hear from the voices in our heads, often when facing new situations or circumstances that would stretch us. At times, those words seem to be literally screaming at us, trying to tell us negative things about ourselves. And sometimes, it is all too easy to listen to them.

Why do we occasionally listen to them, buy into them, and then speak, act, or think as if in agreement with them? I suggest it is because we are sometimes driven by our feared perception of how others *might* view us as opposed to how they actually do. We also fear we could make mistakes, and, of course, if we do, then others will see them.

Not one of us is *ever* insignificant, insecure, not good enough, irrelevant, or underserving. We are all masterpieces, carefully crafted by God to be exactly who we are and who we can become. Our messes, mistakes, trials, and tribulations provide a pathway to the masterpiece God intends each of us to be. The only thing that stops us from thinking that the junkier parts of our lives can go into that masterpiece is listening to negative voices and limiting our faith in ourselves and in God.

The Bible is full of inspiring examples of people who were transformed from junk to productive masterpieces in God's timing.

About Me: Years ago, someone shared with me that each day is an opportunity to build a new past. Although I needed to hear those words, it took me a while to fully grasp their meaning. Being a work in progress as I moved away from the messiness of my past toward spiritual maturity sometimes blinded me to the possible result. But as I leaned less on faith in myself and more on faith in Him, that pinhole of light at the end of the tunnel—hope—became brighter. I can now embrace the fact that I am one of God's masterpieces. It is He who is transforming me, and I am finally quite comfortable in my own skin.

What About You? Is there a person in your life whom you define as great, amazing, totally wonderful—and yet you can't help thinking that even those words aren't descriptive enough? Well, just so you know, God used an incredibly powerful defining word when He created you: masterpiece. You are God's masterpiece. Maybe that definition is a little hard to grasp when life has its moments of going downhill, but you need to know that God is always standing alongside to get you through the tougher times so that you can show yourself confidently with masterpiece status.

Encouraging Words: Genesis 1:26; Ephesians 2:10; Psalm 139:13-14

Spiritual maturity is not how much of the Bible you think you know,
or how well you can recite prayers, but rather,
it is how you act as a person, and use your belief
in a God to better your life and the lives of people around you.
~ Andrew Chong[36]

SOCIAL MEDIA OR ANTISOCIAL MEDIA?

The internet is where some people go to show their true intelligence; others, their hidden stupidity.
~ Criss Jami[37]

Facebook, Twitter, Snapchat, YouTube, Instagram, to name a few. Each fall within the realm of social media. Each can be, and often is, a comfortable means with which to catch up with long-lost friends and relatives, connect with others, share information, find information, enjoy memories, and much, much more. Social media can be a place where folks share or say kind things, funny things, compliments—a place to just be nice toward others. It can be used to bring people together, providing them opportunities to open their hearts to others in kind, pleasant, cordial, polite, and only plain nice conversations.

It is interesting that within the realm of *antisocial* media, we can also list Facebook, Twitter, Snapchat, YouTube, Instagram, and others. These can be, and often are, the means through which one engages in name-calling (often foul), shouting matches in LARGE CAPS, sarcasm, bullying, displays of craziness, swearing, lying, promoting divisiveness, displaying racism and hatred, being intolerant of others, narcissism, and provoking others. It is where one can, without fear of punishment, let out the ugly side of one's heart for all the world to see. There seems to be no limit to the depth of nastiness. Since some social media sites do not require the real name of the word-spewing user, antisocial media provides a platform for keyboard warriors, many of whom seemingly care less about others, about others' feelings, or about others' well-being.

Whether you consider Facebook, Twitter, Snapchat, YouTube, Instagram, and others as social or antisocial media, the sites allow users to be whoever or whatever they are on any given day: nice, not nice; rational, quick-tempered; kind, hateful; deceitful, real. And what about those who do not realize that the more alcohol consumed, the easier it is for ugly to come through the fingers onto the keyboard? Reality is these sites can almost magically draw out the judgmentalism and prejudices of those who try in the real world to keep their negative qualities hidden from others. These sites allow the two-faced to expose each face to the world.

One might wonder if Jesus would use any of them if He were alive today.

About Me: Yes, I am a reformed keyboard warrior. Yes, I have gone ten rounds with the best of them on social media in ugly ways, and I'm not proud of it. Social media did not bring out the worst in me. I already had the worst in me, and social media was a platform where I could and did sometimes show that worst. But when I started a blog page exposing the better side of me, the Jesus-filled side, it dawned on me that I could not have it both ways—a light page and a dark page. I could not live that double standard. And so, I made a choice. Except for marketing efforts for my writing, I have limited my social media use. Life has not only gone on, but it has been much more pleasurable. I still manage to keep up with friends and relatives, the distant ones through e-mails and phone calls (we get pleasure from *talking* to each other). Are all those other friends of the social media platform really friends, or just accumulated numbers? I'll figure that out over time. Am I against the use of social media? For myself, yes. That is because I don't like the me that shows up there at times and says things I later regret saying. It exposes my lack of self-control and my lack of humility to the world. And it has shown me that I have work to do—on myself.

What About You? Is there a possibility that some self-analysis needs to be done regarding your use of social media? Author Kellie Elmore has said that *social media has infected the world with a sickening virus called* *vanity.* Maybe this is the prompting to think about how you can bring your best self into communicating with others.

Encouraging Words: Ephesians 4:31-32; Romans 12:10; James 4:1

Full disclosure here: I have a lot of concerns about social media use—and abuse (as if you couldn't tell already). I have quite a few Christian friends who use and enjoy social media. I also know others who, like me, grit their teeth, grimace, and mutter to themselves later, wondering why they posted what they did. Although some uses of social media can be deemed good, it can be unhealthy spiritually, developmentally, and emotionally. It can be a huge timewaster, as was the case with me. Numerous studies show it can have terribly negative effects on our youth and their social development. I have seen that first-hand as I have watched some bubbling, outgoing kids turn into withdrawn, socially inept, self-absorbed youths with smart phones glued to their hands as if held there by an umbilical cord. That is scary. One might say it is a parenting problem when parents lack the guts to limit phone use or take away the phone altogether.

Following is a series of quotes reflecting much of my thinking about social media. I share these additional observations primarily because I sense that a lot of people have perhaps innocently allowed themselves to get swallowed up by the supposed importance of social media and, in doing so, have lost some of the realness of who they are as a part of God's creation. Some readers may disagree, and I am okay with that. Perhaps we can simply agree to disagree and move on. (You can go onto your favorite search engine to find out more about any of the comment-givers below.)

It is not entirely healthy for adults or children: *In the last 10 years, we have seen a rise in selfishness: selfies, self-absorbed people, superficiality, self-degradation, apathy, and self-destruction. So, I challenge all of you to take initiative to change this programming. Instead of celebrating the ego, let's flip the script and celebrate the heart. Let's put the ego and celebrity culture to sleep and awaken the conscience. This is the battle we must all fight together to win back our humanity. To save our future, and our children.* ~ Suzy Kassem[38]

Social media infatuation can diminish our social skills: *Our social tools are not an improvement to modern society. They are a challenge to it.* ~ Clay Shirky[39]

It can have a negative effect on our desire for humility: *It amazes me that we are all on Twitter and Facebook. By "we" I mean adults. We're adults, right? But emotionally we're a culture of seven-year-olds. Have you ever had that moment when you are updating your status and you realize that every status update is just a variation on a single request: "Would someone please acknowledge me?"* ~ Mark Maron[40]

It feeds our ego and diminishes our reliance on God for joy: *An open Facebook page is simply a psychiatric dry erase board that screams, "Look at me. I am insecure. I need your reaction to what I am doing, but you're not cool enough to be my friend. Therefore, I will pray you see this because the approval of God is not all I need."* ~ Shannon L. Alder[41]

It can, through overexposure, dull our sensibilities and values: *If you don't like pictures of animal cruelty being posted on social media, you need to stop the cruelty, not the pictures. You should be bothered that it's happening, not that you saw it.* ~ Marie Sarantakis[42]

It can diminish our sense of empathy and compassion for others: *People get addicted to feeling offended all the time because it gives them a high; being self-righteous and morally superior feels good.* ~ Mark Manson[43]

It is addictive to many, and as such, it can control one's time and focus about matters of living real: *The tycoons of social media have to stop pretending that they're friendly nerd gods building a better world and admit they're just tobacco farmers in T-shirts selling an addictive product to children. Because, let's face it, checking your "likes" is the new smoking.* ~ Cal Newport[44]

It can be a breeding ground for narcissism and a sense of false self-importance: *Almost universally, the kind of performance we give on social media is positive. It's more "Let me tell you how well things are going. Look how great I am." It's rarely the truth: "I'm scared. I'm struggling. I don't know."* ~ Ryan Holiday[45]

It can show the real condition of our heart toward others when we use it wrong: *If you are on social media, and you are not learning, not laughing, not being inspired or not networking, then you are using it wrong.* ~ Germany Kent[46]

It can easily let us fall into the trap of taking everything/ everyone at its word by inhibiting our ability to think things through: *How easy it is for so many of us today to be undoubtedly full of information yet fully deprived of accurate information.* ~ Criss Jami[47]

What About You (one more time)? Have you considered the negatives about social media regarding your usage of it? How many of the above statements apply to you, even in some small way? Would you consider that a red flag? If you have already limited your usage of social media, or simply dropped away from it in favor of spending your time more wisely, you deserve a pat on the back.

IT'S AMAZING

I have given Christ countless reasons not to love me.
None of them have changed His mind.
~ Paul Washer[48]

From my perspective as a believer in God a follower of Christ, and one trying to live a Christian life, I am struck by how quickly my demeanor can shift between positives and negatives. Maybe you can relate, even if you are not sure about how or whether God is touching your life.

It's amazing—the quiet moments with God, when our heads are in sync with our hearts and all is well.

It's amazing—how quickly moments with God fall apart when something from our worldview intrudes and that synchronicity disappears in a flash.

It's amazing—how it feels when we listen to that small, still voice deep within our hearts and recognize it for what it is: God sharing His voice with us.

It's amazing—how we can turn away from that voice in an instant and respond to the voice from the evil one yelling in our mind, and how quickly we yield to that one.

It's amazing—how we bolster up so much resolve to live as He would have us live, only to have that resolve crushed so quickly as we succumb to temptations.

It's amazing—how quickly we become contrite and horrified at what we have done, said, or thought and return to His presence to seek forgiveness.

It's amazing—this yo-yo life we live, with its ups and downs. But it is nowhere near as amazing as the magnitude of God's grace and redemption as we struggle continuously with ourselves, our inner conflicts, our doubts, our fears, our passions, and our sin along the road called life.

It's amazing—how blessed we truly are.

About Me: I felt conflicted for a long time. I wanted to live my Christian life right but could not shake saying or doing dumb, stupid, sinful things—and then beating myself up because of them. Nowadays, I find that I still say and do dumb, stupid, and sinful things. But now I have a deep appreciation of, and have grasped the depth of, His grace and redemption and what it means for me. His forgiveness enables me to forgive myself and acknowledge to myself that as a broken man, I have a sinful nature that I will never eliminate. That same forgiveness (His) prompts me to try to get it right again and again and again. I smile in amazement that He continues to love as I keep on trying, and it bolsters my perception that God is all about the progress as I strive for unattainable perfection.

What About You? Do you find it frustrating, perhaps sometimes futile, when you think about the yo-yo life you experience? Are you as amazed by the good within you as you are by the not-so-good? Do you seek to shift perspectives by relying on your own strength, or do you think about allowing in a Higher Power? It is amazing the impact God's grace and love can have in your life.

Encouraging Words: Philippians 2:13

A PEBBLE IN THE SHOE

The most effective way to share the gospel is to live it.
When we live like disciples of Christ should live,
when we aren't just good but happy to be good,
others will be drawn to us.
~ Sheri L. Dew[49]

Some things in life are just plain uncomfortable. One example is going to the bathroom in the dark of night and inadvertently stepping on one of your kid's Legos. Equally uncomfortable is having a pebble in your shoe. The pebble nags at you until you stop what you are doing to get it out.

These two uncomfortable things have a lot in common with how Christians sometimes conduct themselves in relationships with non-believers—that discomfort being with a person who is obnoxiously in-your-face when sharing their love of the Lord. Just in the way any of us live our life is a witness to our beliefs and values; it is called witnessing when Christians share their faith beliefs with others. We must remember that how others perceive us through our words and actions can impact a person's decision regarding their own spiritual future.

If a Christian's witnessing effort comes across as a complete surprise (as in the Lego example), the recipient of that effort may likely look at the witnessing as just another passing fancy. However, if the witnessing effort is an in-your-face style, it can become very uncomfortable for the recipient, and most likely doors will shut...in your face. But when a Christian's witnessing effort is predicated on their daily actions and words (and heart) consistently showing a quality example of a godly life, their witness becomes like the pebble in the shoe. It tends to nag on the person wearing the shoe until he or she sorts things out and does something about it.

About Me: What captured the heart of this formerly hard-boiled non-believer were several pebbles in my shoe. Those pebbles were folks who were living as Jesus with skin on and feet to the ground here on earth. They were literally living their eulogy with little to no effort to get in my face. Accepting me as I was at the time, they let their life examples do most of the talking for them. When it was time for me to start asking questions, they were there patiently with answers that I could understand at the level I was at.

What About You? If you are a Christian, are you are spiritually on fire, and do you let your life example be your witness to others? Are you equipped to be the pebble in someone's shoe? If you are a non-Christian reading this, have you had that pebble in the shoe? What did you choose to do about it?

Encouraging Words: John 1:8; 1 Peter 3:15; Matthew 5:16; Colossians 4:2-6

LESSONS FROM AN EGRET

The happiest man is he who learns from nature the lesson of worship.
~ Ralph Waldo Emerson[50]

E grets. Loners, long and lanky, regal looking, beautiful. Persistent, reliant on their instincts, patient, cautious, and, yes, cunning to a degree. I was fascinated as I watched an egret one day. There it was, patiently doing exactly what they all must do to survive—stalk for food. That big bird would strut deliberately and very slowly in the shallows of the pond, one cautious step after another, its head pivoting back and forth in search for that next bit of food (a fish, frog, or bug) which would comprise part of its meal for that time of day.

About Me: As I watched that egret, I realized it was an example of God's gift of nature to me. Was there something I could learn from it?

- The egret was reliant on its God-given ability to provide for itself. Me: Often, I'm far too reliant on myself. I don't know if egrets are in union with God or not (though I don't doubt that they are of God), but I concluded that if I were truly reliant on God for *everything*, I would surely survive. He would never fail to meet my needs (not necessarily my wants) just as He meets the egret's needs.
- The egret was certainly persistent and patient. No patience, no eats—simple as that. Me: I considered how impatient I tend to be and how that impatience usually has a negative effect on my life. Persistence? It is easy at times for me to give up or to tire of

what I may be doing, so I quit. That lack of persistence affects my spiritual life at times in that it is easy to become lazy, bored, tired, distracted. And then I lose focus. Unlike the egret, who is engaged in full-metal mental focus to feed his body, feeding my soul doesn't always get my fully focused attention.

- The egret was overly cautious as it stalked its prey, taking slow, deliberate, well-planned steps as it searched for its next bite. Me: I considered how I proceed in my spiritual journey. Sometimes, it is the shotgun approach with buckshot scattered all over the place. Sometimes, it is the reckless, full-bore, no-holds-barred approach. Sometimes, it is just spurts here and there with no real plan. But occasionally, it is a thoughtful, planned, and organized approach such that I can fully receive and feel the feeding that just took place. The difference between the egret and myself is that he is consistent in his approach and quest for sustenance and I'm not.

Perhaps the egret being there that day was part of God's plan for me. Though the egret's sole purpose was simply to fish for his meal, it became a model for me to think about some life lessons I needed at that moment in time. I learned some lessons from the teacher (the egret) and his routine.

What About You? Are you tuned in to allow nature (all of which is from God) to teach you things you may need in your life or on your spiritual journey? Allow nature to be yet another provision from God for your learning experiences, and let it provide relatable lessons to learn from.

Encouraging Words: Job 12:7-10

A MORNING PRAYER

Lord, I want to make this a full day of fellowship.

With You.

Every waking hour.

You are with me always.

I am the one who ignores that all too often.

So today, Lord, the whole day, gently remind me, as often as I need it, that You are in fellowship with me and I with You.

When those moments come, and they always do, that I get distracted by those necessary things of this worldly life, help me to remember that even in those times, we are in fellowship, and to act accordingly.

In those other moments, when all is quiet, help me to enjoy those quiet moments of fellowship with You because You are still with me.

And Lord, as the day closes and I prepare for a time of rest, help me to praise You in deep thankfulness for another day shared in fellowship with You.

Lord, I pray for a full day of fellowship.

With You.

Every waking hour.

Amen.

~ Joe Miller

ROCKS RISING

God who lives in you gives you the grace
to move beyond your deepest wounds and say,
"You are forgiven" and "I am forgiven."
If you allow Him, He will give you a fresh start—right now.
~ Sue Augustine[51]

Anyone who has ever tilled the soil knows all about rocks, large and small. At the nursery where I work, the laborers are constantly removing rocks and boulders, not all of which were visible when the fields were tilled. Rocks and boulders tend to rise to the surface due to changing weather conditions, particularly so during the winter months. Farmers are very aware of the nuisance those rocks, and boulders can be to their equipment.

We humans, like the fields, have rocks and boulders within us. They weigh us down at times, and when they rise to the surface, we are not always nice in our responses. Our attitudes suffer, and we can become closed off or aloof toward others. The rocks and boulders we carry within us represent the past junk we want to keep hidden rather than facing it and dealing with it, the junk that drives us at times. That junk can include such things as real or perceived slights, long-ignored anger that keeps festering and raising its ugly head, or past hurts (real or imagined), among other things.

Our rocks are burdens. We don't have to carry them, yet many of us do, and for a long time. Just as farmland and nurseries need to be tilled, we need to till ourselves. If we fail to get rid of our rocks and boulders as they rise to the surface, they will continue to weigh us down and will continue to impact our responses and reactions to situations and people. Those rocks will continue to block the pathway to our heart that we need for a healthy and solid relationship with our Lord. By not disposing of our rocks, we stand little chance of being free and being the people God intended us to be.

So how do we best relieve ourselves of those rising rocks? First, we identify them as rocks and acknowledge they are there. Then we talk with a trusted Christian brother(s) or sister(s) about the impact of those rocks on us. Alongside that, we must seek and extend forgiveness, including to ourselves. Finally, we must remind ourselves that those rocks will not define us. What will define us is that we are children of God.

About Me: My personal rock pile was much larger and had been around much longer than I even knew. After being led to give identity to those rocks, I was able to clearly see just how much they had defined me and weighed me down over the years. Gratefully, I experienced how getting rid of those rocks opened my heart to much more freedom than I ever would have imagined.

What About You? What kind of burdens of the past are you still carrying, and to what degree do they define you as a person? Are you even aware of *all* the rocks and boulders you carry? If you wonder why you react and respond to people and situations as you sometimes do, could it be because some of those rocks keep rising? Take time and counsel to rid yourself of those impeding rocks so that you can move on to the fresh start God wants for you.

Encouraging Words: Matthew 11:28-30; Galatians 6:2; John 16:33; Psalm 145:14

OUR DIET

Every day God invites us on the same kind of adventure.
It's not a trip where He sends us a rigid itinerary,
He simply invites us. God asks what it is He's made us to love,
what it is that captures our attention, what feeds that deep indescribable
need of our souls to experience the richness of the world He made.
And then, leaning over us, He whispers, "Let's go do that together."
~ Bob Goff[52]

D iet. The word means different things to different people. Those of us who think about our future health usually plan meals and snacks around healthy foods. For those who have gained weight, the word "diet" brings thoughts not just of eating healthy foods, but of eating less at each sitting. Whatever the case, diet is not limited to what we put into our mouths.

Our diets consist not only of food, but what we watch, what we listen to, what we read, and who we hang around with. Whatever we put into our bodies and minds becomes part of our daily diet. Therefore, we need to be very mindful of what we consume, not just physically, but emotionally and spiritually as well.

If we neglect ingesting good, healthy food and try to thrive on junk food, we will become undernourished or fat, each with its own physical ramifications. If on a consistent basis we watch junk, listen to junk, read junk, and surround ourselves with junk, we tend to become junk. Our emotional and spiritual lives suffer.

About Me: Food has never been an issue with me. Though I have never paid a lot of attention to what and how much I eat, overall, my body has always responded well, and I've always been healthy and within medical limits for the most part. It was the other stuff on my diet—drugs, alcohol, gambling, and poor sexual values—particularly in the earlier years of my life, that wreaked havoc on relationships, my emotional health, and my spiritual life. The single most important thing I needed in my diet throughout those years was something that was not in it— any semblance of a Christian life and Christian community. I thank God that I changed my diet to include a strong, committed community of fellow believers.

What About You? Do you need to change your diet in any areas of your life? In what ways is some, or all, of what you ingest having a negative effect on your physical, emotional, and/or spiritual life? What can you do about that? Think about changes you can make. There is an abundance of healthy "food" out there that can bring life change—physically, emotionally, spiritually. Enjoy.

Encouraging Words: Proverbs 13:20; Proverbs 27:17; Psalm 1:1-3; 1 Corinthians 6:19-20

IT WON'T HAPPEN TO ME

*The devil wants to stop any believer
from fulfilling his or her God-given destiny.
He also knows that most believers feel
almost vulnerable after a mountaintop experience with God.
Actually, that's when we are most vulnerable
because falling into sin is the last thing we are expecting.
We're wise to expect times of testing after times of blessing.*
~ Beth Moore[53]

The attitude of feeling invincible has few boundaries. Many of the younger generation often display that attitude, but it isn't limited to them. Case in point, and a true story:

He was a sixty-four-year-old male of Jewish descent, divorced for approximately eight years. At his arrival to our small group about four years ago under some seemingly odd circumstances, it was obvious that he had some major issues in all aspects of his life. God and a strong community of guys stepped up to the plate, and within a couple of years, he accepted Jesus Christ as his Lord and Savior, got baptized, and became an integral part of the group. It was exhilarating to see the heart changes taking place within him. He became vibrant, was open and transparent and fairly content, given his bleak financial circumstances. He was easy to love, and he shared his love for others. That lasted for a couple of years. And then things changed.

He stopped coming to church and group. Texts and calls became sporadic, and sometimes sardonic. It was clear that something was going on in this guy's life, but he rebuked any opportunities to be transparent and engage in other than meaningless conversations. It was also quite evident that he was hurting inside, yet he was quick to set boundaries on conversations when there were visits from any of his brothers.

During a four-month period, he let anyone who would listen know that he was in dire straits financially. He had always been on a financial tightrope, especially in the early years of his connection with our group, and it was not uncommon that the guys, individually or sometimes collectively, would help him out. As he grew spiritually, his financial situation seemed to stabilize, so when he started to share his dire straits once again, things just did not add up. Yet he would not talk about it. Given his stated financial condition, it came as a shock when he opened enough to inform us that he was moving out of state.

Several days before his supposed move date, he gathered a couple of brothers because he implied that he wanted to come clean and stop hiding the truth about what was going on. When he started his so-called confession with the statement that he was not afraid of dying, but that he feared dying alone, red flags flew all over the place. He explained that for the past four months, he had become heavily involved with pornography (something he had admittedly dabbled in previously), and that led to heavy involvement with some internet dating sites. Hooking up online and texting with a series of out-of-state "females," who supposedly really cared for him, led him to feel that he could become serious with them.

The irony is that they all, for an assortment of reasons, needed money, which he sent, such that for three months he could not make his rent payments or his car payments. He also took out loans totaling over $25,000 to meet the supposed needs of these online contacts. This mess with finances led to him being evicted and put out on the streets. His out-of-state move never took place, because, of course, it was one of those dating site parasites who had convinced him there was a place for him—if he would just send the necessary rent deposit for the two of them.

So, this once seemingly healthy guy is now out on the streets, his belongings tossed to the curb by the Sheriff's Department eviction unit. Where this will all end is anyone's guess. His back is still turned, even though his brothers have remained steadfast in their spiritual encouragement.

The point of this discussion is to bring home the fallacy of the attitude "it won't happen to me." Here is why. In a nutshell, three things happened:

- Satan went for the weak spot and gained a threshold in the man.
- As a result, this guy made some bad choices and unwise decisions.
- Those bad choices led to an outcome that was very, very ugly.

At this point, only God knows what the outcome will be.

About Me: As I've taken time to identify my weaknesses and vulnerabilities (which we all have), I have realized that they are the doorways through which Satan can enter my heart and mind and take me down if I'm not constantly on guard against such. I do not want to *ever* think it won't happen to me, because it can—at any time, just as it has in the past. In the case of my friend, his response to the initial dabbling in pornography was that it was just a once in a while an occasional thing. It was not. His retort to later discussion about heavier involvement was "it won't happen to me." It did. And I realize I am no less vulnerable.

What About You? Is your heart and relationship with God worth the gamble of some negative, whatever that is, happening to you? Do you know how to guard the doorways within you from Satan? Are you doing enough? Allow others of integrity within your community to come alongside and stand strong for and with you.

Encouraging Words: Proverbs 4:23; Colossians 3:5; 1 Thessalonians 4:1-8; Jeremiah 17:10; Ephesians 6:10-11

The astonishing paradox of Christ's teaching
and of Christian experience is this:
if we lose ourselves in following Christ,
we actually find ourselves.
True self-denial is self-discovery.
To live for ourselves is insanity and suicide;
to live for God and for man is wisdom and life indeed.
We do not begin to find ourselves until we have become willing
to lose ourselves in the service of Christ and of our fellows.
~ John R. W. Stott[54]

FAIR WARNING

Sometimes you make choices in life and sometimes choices make you.
~ Gayle Forman[55]

We appreciate a sense of fairness in others, don't we? Most of us probably think of ourselves as fair-minded people and generally expect it of others. We do not wake up in the morning and plan to be mean-spirited, vindictive people who react adversely to the smallest slight. But what about when we do act in that manner? When someone or something comes at us that we feel is not justified, we react. We are all guilty of not being fair sometimes. And I wonder if we realize how fair God <u>always</u> is.

In 1934, Cole Porter penned the words for what became a well-known song and musical. *Anything Goes* was a masterpiece. If you read the song lyrics, you get the sense that, well, anything goes, especially in the world in which we live today. And if you are like me, you may wonder and may be concerned about our world as we know it in today's times.

As we consider the moral decay and declining spiritual values in our society (and, indeed, in the world), don't we sometimes wonder where God fits into that picture? If He is a fair God, how can all of this be happening in the world that He created?

When God created man, He gave man the ability to make choices. And the problem centers on the choices we sometimes make. Some of the many choices we make are not good ones. And the more we have that *anything goes* mindset, the poorer choices we are likely to make.

A hard look at history—societies that have fallen, biblical prophecies, current events— provides us with a picture of not only what we are in today's times, but why we are as we are as a society. A specific look at Scripture shows us that God *is* fair. He gave us noticeably clear and fair warning of the consequences of the choices we make. That warning should serve to dampen our "anything goes" attitude. Unfortunately, we still make bad choices.

The world, and our society, will only change if we, as individuals, change. Individually, we must decide that the fair warning God gave us is worth the effort to change.

About Me: A good look at my past would show you that I lived by "anything goes." My mantra was "the greater the risk, the greater the reward," and I neglected to consider the little things called consequences that automatically come with bad decisions and bad choices—often, painfully so. As a non-Christian, I figured a fair warning automatically gave someone else an edge over me. And I felt I was never given fair warning. But along my spiritual journey, I have come to accept, understand, and embrace God's true character. He has never wavered in His warning to humanity, me included, what the consequences will be for not following His Word. That is completely fair and helps me to make the right decisions and choices. It is all there in God's Word, in black and white, consistent and truthful, with no wiggle room.

What About You? Have your values succumbed to "anything goes"? Do you recognize how yielding to lessened spiritual values will influence you and what the ultimate effect of lessened values could have on your outlook and actions? Do you understand the potential consequences when your mind tells you it is okay because "anything goes"? Rather than giving in, let God's Word be your manual for living.

Encouraging Words: Romans 1:18-32

TO MY GRANDCHILD

The truth is, unless you let go,
unless you forgive yourself,
unless you forgive the situation,
unless you realize that the situation is over,
you cannot move forward.
~ Steve Maraboli[56]

Dear Grandchild,
Christmas tends to be a melancholy time for me. I saw a meme a bit back, and it brought a flashflood of painful memories. Many years ago, during the Christmas season, my stepdaughter's boyfriend gave me an expensive bottle of scotch as a Christmas gift. I recall that I found it odd and I was not very comfortable with the idea, since they were both seniors in high school. I also recall that he seemed quite ill at ease during the conversation we had that day, and I was baffled by his demeanor. I had the feeling that something was up, but because there was nothing in our conversation to indicate what it might have been, I chalked it up to a nervous boyfriend taking a stab at brown-nosing me. Little did I realize what was really going on.

After the Christmas break, when school was back in session, I inadvertently found out the horrid truth. It was a secret that I was not supposed to become aware of. Over the break, my stepdaughter had not gone to visit with friends for a week—or so I had been told. Rather, she had gone to the city to abort you. I wasn't even aware that she was pregnant. That news was kept from me. I assume that was easy because I was busy working two jobs to support our family of seven kids. Although I

96

was not a Christian at the time, my wife knew that I opposed abortion, even though I tended to be somewhat liberal in my views.

Since I was an active alcoholic then, perhaps my tendency toward erratic and angry outbursts were a factor in the secretiveness of their decision not to include me in the process. During that year, I tried to discuss the issue in a non-accusatory and loving manner with my wife, but the door to that conversation was slammed shut almost immediately. It was one of those "I don't want to talk about that" conversations. The response only revived the sense of hurt I felt over what I saw as an unhealthy relationship. I could not put together the logic that someone being a professed Catholic embraced abortion any more than I could understand the need for the secrecy.

Over the ensuing years (as I write this, it's now thirty-eight), I have often wondered if you were a boy or a girl, and what kind of man or woman you would have grown up to be. I've also wondered if my step-daughter simply chalked the abortion off as a passing necessity, or if she has likewise wondered how you would have turned out whether she had kept you or put you up for adoption. Those are things I will never know. I have chosen, over the years, to keep the matter to myself because of the shallowness of the relationship we seem to have had. Attempts to improve the relationship have been difficult, though on-going, and progress has been extremely slow.

And so, as another Christmas season looms, I once again find myself wondering about things like what you would look like now, what your personality would be like, would you have children and what would they be like—basically, just what kind of life you would have lived. Yes, they are all just questions, but ones that never really go away because you, dear one, never had a chance or any say in the matter—just like me. It's sad, isn't it?

Grampa

About Me: The above is a true story. Fortunately, and happily, I ultimately became a Christian. God's Word has taught me many things about relationships and helped me to grow in forgiveness, grace, patience, tolerance, and, most of all, trust in Him. I have learned that though I may not like my circumstances, God indeed has His plan for me. It may be one I do not like or one whose outcome I must wait on. I have also learned that despite my circumstances, I am called to be His light in all that I say and do. And I must remember that once upon a time, it was only because of some others who were His light that a crusty, hard-hearted man such as myself could find the way, the truth, and the light. An important life lesson I learned was the power of forgiveness, to others and to myself.

What About You? Have you found yourself in hard, disturbing, and perhaps ugly circumstances in relationships? Do you find it difficult to trust God for the outcomes? Does your faith falter at those times? How do you handle it? My prayer is that you find others who will come alongside any time you need to figure out the forgiveness thing as a first step for healing.

Encouraging words: Jeremiah 29:11-14; Romans 12:2; 1 Timothy 5:8; Matthew 6:25-34

A REAL DEAL

Things which matter most must never be
at the mercy of things which matter least.
~ Johann Wolfgang von Goethe[57]

It was recently reported that a pair of Michael Jordan's game-worn shoes from the 1984 Olympics were sold at auction for, *gasp*, $190,373! That is a lot of money for a pair of foot-sweat-soaked shoes. And what makes it even more astonishing is that Jordan was not even in the NBA or the winner of six championships at the time he wore those shoes.

One may wonder about the priorities of a person willing to shell out that kind of money for a pair of used shoes. But we likely will never know because typically that level of buyer has a private side that is not easily researched. When I read about this purchase, my thoughts went to how much goodwell that amount of money could do if spent in a needy neighborhood or community. I wondered if the shoe buyer ever spent money like that in a private and quiet manner for the good of mankind.

Is it wrong to wonder about someone who spends that kind of money for a pair of used shoes? Is it judgmental to question how anyone spends their money? If a person questions another's priorities and possible relationship with the Lord, is that being critical? Is there all that much difference between how the average person and all others do life, other than the degrees of money involved? Wouldn't the same questions apply?

Reality is, it is all about priorities, and in the end, all of our priorities come under scrutiny by God, so what any of us may think about a deal on a pair of shoes doesn't really matter. Many of us know that by far the most valuable things we can ever get—grace and freedom—come because of Jesus on the cross. Neither costs $190,373, nor neither stinks like used shoes. Both are free, just by claiming Him. Now that is a real deal.

About Me: I plead guilty to a jaded sense of priorities in earlier years. I was a hyper-active collector of anything related to Dale Earnhardt, Sr., of NASCAR fame. My collection was both extreme and expensive. I often spent money I could ill afford to get that next collectable because it was a real deal. I did not think of better, less worldly places all that money could have been spent. Years later, after becoming a Christian, and only after having sold the collection at a rather considerable loss, did I begin to grasp the fact that stuff is just that—stuff. And what I had spent on my stuff could have been used for any number of Kingdom causes.

What About You? Like me, perhaps you have spent money on some collection or item or experience that seemed totally rational at the time, but that you now reflect on as not a wise decision. And you have maybe also questioned how others have spent their money on what you deem weird or worthless stuff. With all the need in our world, maybe you can find a worthy cause, Kingdom or otherwise, in which you can make a difference by your support.

Encouraging Words: Matthew 16:26; Deuteronomy 15:11; 1 John 3:17-18

A BUZZARD, BAT,
AND A BUMBLEBEE

Look upward to your God for direction!
Look inward into yourself and discover your talents!
Look outward into your environment and get helped!
Stop looking in one direction!
~ Israelmore Ayivor[58]

If you put a buzzard in a 6' x 8' pen that is entirely open at the top, the bird, despite its marvelous ability to fly and soar, will be an absolute prisoner. The reason is that a buzzard always begins its flight from the ground with a run of 10 to 12 feet. Without space to run, as is its habit, it will not even attempt to fly but will remain a prisoner in a small jail cell with no top.

The ordinary bat, which flies around at night and is a remarkably nimble creature in the air, cannot take off from a level place. If a bat is placed on the floor or on flat ground, all it can do is shuffle about helplessly and, no doubt, painfully, until it reaches a slight elevation from which it can throw itself into the air. Then, at once, it takes off like a flash.

A bumblebee, if dropped into an open tumbler, will be there until it dies. Unless taken out manually, the bee never sees the means of escape at the open top and will persist in trying to find some way out through the sides near the bottom. That bumblebee will seek a way where none exists, until it eventually destroys itself.

In many ways, we are like the buzzard, the bat, and the bumblebee. We struggle with our various problems and frustrations, often without realizing that all we need to do is look up...to Him! That is going vertical...to Him.

About Me: I am no different than many folks. I have lived a large part of my life with the mind-set of "I've got this." Sometimes, I was successful in squeezing myself out of the box I had put myself in, but even in those times, the end results were often temporary. As a controlling type of person, I had to control situations just as much as I had to control people. I viewed it as "engineered results." In that darker period of my life, I viewed God as one who had a large foot that was going to squash me if I messed up bad. I never considered Him as a kind, loving, compassionate, personal friend I could reach to vertically for help. It never dawned on me that had I done so, He would have said, "I got this, son."

What About You? Are you like a buzzard, bat, or bumblebee, failing to look up when faced with problems and frustrations? Next time you feel trapped, look up, yield control to God, spread your wings, and fly.

Encouraging Words: Psalm 25; James 1:5-6

CONVICTIONS

*Following Christ isn't something that can be done
halfheartedly or on the side. It is not a label we can display when
it is useful. It must be central to everything we do and are.*
~ Francis Chan[59]

When I grew up, boxing was in its prime. A young boxer came onto the scene in those days, and in many minds, he went on to become one of the greatest boxers of all time. His name was Cassius Clay. I loved watching him on our little black-and-white TV. He was cagey, fast, and he could slug. I did not like much else about him, though, because he was brash, outspoken, arrogant, and boastful.

When Cassius Clay changed his name to Muhammad Ali, my respect for him sagged further. He put the nail in the coffin for any remaining respect I had for him when he openly and publicly resisted the draft. (There was a military draft back then, and this was during the time when Viet Nam was cranking up.) Many were dodging the draft in those days, and some whom I knew ran away to Canada to avoid it. To many of us, those draft-dodgers were worse than black sheep.

For years, I despised Ali for being so brazen about draft-dodging. Only when he died in 2017 did my thinking about him change. I learned that his personal conviction about the draft cost him personally. His decision had cost him an absolute ton, along with all the public disdain and loss of respect people like me heaped on him. I had not paid attention to that stuff earlier because my only focus was on disliking him because he had dodged the draft.

Why am I sharing this? Because even though I disagreed with him (and thus disliked him because of the choices he made), I concluded, after fully understanding what his personal convictions truly cost him, that I should respect him. He did something few of us ever do. He stood tall on his convictions while facing enormous costs to himself and his family. Much like the apostle Paul in the Bible, Ali stood by his convictions while facing the wrath of the world around him. Unlike many of us in these modern times who are so motivated or led by political correctness and our worldviews, neither Paul nor Ali were afraid to stand on their convictions.

And so, for those of us who claim Christianity, maybe we need to ask ourselves these questions regarding our convictions:

- Am I reluctant to share my faith publicly and boldly with others?
- Am I willing to take any heat or ridicule for being openly Christian?
- Do I show my reliance on Christ in my life as an example of biblical living?
- Do I really have spiritual convictions?

Convictions—easy to yak about, sometimes hard to live. Inspirational author Shannon L. Alder perhaps says it best when she reminds us, *Your religion is not what you do on Sunday. It is how you live Monday through Saturday.*

About Me: Ali's decision, based on his convictions, was a lived decision, day in and day out, for the rest of his life. He not only talked the talk but walked the walk. His has been a good example for me to not only have my own convictions, but to live them, day in and day out—and to pick myself up when I fail.

What About You? How did you answer those questions asked above? Like Ali, it's important to know your convictions, to know what influenced those convictions, and to stand strong in those convictions.

Encouraging Words: Hebrews 11:1; Galatians 2:20; Luke 16:13

DIFFICULT RELATIONSHIPS

It isn't as bad as you sometimes think it is.
It all works out. Don't worry.
I say that to myself every morning.
It all works out in the end.
Put your trust in God and move forward
with faith and confidence in the future.
The Lord will not forsake us. If we will put our trust in Him,
if we will pray to Him, if we will live worthy of His blessings,
He will hear our prayers.
~ Gordon B. Hinkley[60]

I t was the doggonedest thing (to share a bad pun). They had taken in a rescue fur baby over a year ago. She was an exceptionally well-behaved gal and took right to the family. Well, almost. She began a wonderful love relationship with the lady of the house immediately. It had been reciprocal love at first sight, a love that strengthened each day. It was also love at first sight from the man of the house, but it was decidedly not reciprocal. The pooch was completely leery of him from the get-go, to the point that she would not be in the same room as him. Perhaps her former life held a sad history that dictated how she felt and acted toward males. Over the course of that first year, there were wee-tiny signs of progress in her warming up to him, but it was very tenuous and painfully slow. This, even though he was the one who walked her, gave her car rides (which she was crazy about), fed her, and loved on her consistently as much as she decided to allow him. The emotional scars she carried were evidently deeply rooted, to the point where it was not uncommon for him to wonder if she would ever show typical dog love toward him. It was a somewhat difficult relationship for him. But he was patient.

During this same time, the man of the house was involved in another somewhat difficult relationship. This one was with his wife of many decades. The "once upon a time" period of their lives was long gone, and to him, it often seemed as if the "happily ever after" might never occur. Along the way, they had experienced some happy times, some sad times, some good times, and some bad times—no different than any other marriage. But heaped across all those times was the fact that this couple was unevenly yoked spiritually. The husband also felt that the web of older age was affecting her much more than him—such that he was concerned that perhaps she was in a somewhat depressed state and possibly in the early stages of dementia. Some typical signs of this difficult form of elder diminishment were evident, so, yes, he was concerned. What little love language his wife had once spoken was slowly diminishing. Some of her actions were not quite as normal or as usual for what had, at one time, been a bright and outgoing lady. Her thought processes were changing, as were her ways of communicating. As his role seemed to be slowly shifting from that of companion to that of caretaker, the husband wondered at times if his wife would ever again show the love for him that he had once felt. It had become a somewhat difficult relationship for him. But he was patient.

With both dog and wife, the man felt a lack of love and, to a degree, lack of meaningful companionship, which was something he hungered for, something he was used to. It was something not given routinely in the dog and man example, and something taken away by circumstance in the husband and wife example. The lack of relationship played a key role in both relationships, and each was difficult for him. In neither example could it be said that the man had any culpability in the situation. The former's cause was attributed to emotional canine scars which followed the dog in rescue. The latter's cause was partly the curse of time, and most certainly, medical issues. All three—the dog, the wife, and the husband—were victims.

Interestingly, the compelling truth contained within each example is not the victimhood of the people or the dog. Nor is it either of the specific tragedies as they played out. In each of the examples, the compelling truth falls squarely within the realm of "that's life" and how the man chose to deal with each situation.

About Me: Since the above examples are about me, I would like to share some other compelling truths:

- I was not, and am not, always patient. There have been times when I wanted to find another home for the dog because of the way she is. There have also been times when my fantasy run-to runaway spot beckons me strongly as the weight of the home situation and the future I imagine leans into me. There have been plenty of times when I have cried, sometimes out loud, "Why me?" There have also been times when I have thought, *I don't deserve this.* And there have been times when I have fully tried to step into the role of fixer, even knowing that I alone cannot do it. There have also been times when I was mad at God for my lot in life. I mean, why can't I have that happily ever after all the fairy tales remind us about in our formative youth? Each of these thoughts and feelings shows my humanness. They also show a measure of my brokenness.

- Those examples also show another human side of me—a good side. Each shows a willingness, outside of some weaker moments, to accept circumstances as they are and to lean into patience and understanding. Each shows I grasp the concept that life is not always fair, and I choose to be okay with that.

- I am a firm believer that God's hand is all over my life and has never not been. I passionately believe that God's hand is a guiding hand and a molding hand, taking me places He knows I need in my life. In that vein, who am I to question Him? I am completely aware that I need to learn more about patience. And tolerance. And unconditional love. And humility. And gratefulness (I know many others have it much worse than I do). I need to learn to live like Jesus, with skin on. I do believe that I am squarely where God wants me, doing what He wants me to do. And I am not doing it to pay my dues toward heaven. I am doing it because of His two commands to love God and love your neighbor (which includes anyone and anything besides myself). *Those* are compelling mandates.

What About You? How do circumstances beyond your control, particularly adversarial or difficult ones and especially long-term ones, affect you? How do your reactions and choices affect your relationships? Are there any compelling truths you might need to figure out and apply to your life? Take time to appreciate your humanness when it shows up and reign it in when it wants to take you places you know not to be right. Lean into God's teachings about living life His way as a source of strength during those times.

Encouraging Words: 2 Corinthians 4:8-9, 1 Peter 5:10, Joshua 1:9, James 1:2-4

SQUANDERED

The good choices we didn't make clearly show how much of our lives was squandered. When I look in the mirror, I see me. And I think.
~ Joe Miller

I mportant moments in time. Opportunities. Family bonds. Friendships. Job advancements. Time with kids growing up. Dreams and hopes. Future financial security. Trust and respect. One's own potential. Self-esteem. Changed hearts. A lot of unknowns. One's well-being and health.

About Me: That is a list of some of the pieces of my life that I squandered because I failed to make good choices during my journey from childhood well into adulthood. Unfortunately, many of my choices were based on worldly thinking rather than spiritually grounded thinking. I eventually learned to define good choices as godly, wise choices, choices that positively affect or affected not just myself, but also those around me.

So, yes, there was the bad news. But the good news is that here in the winter of my life, I have come to know a God of compassion and forgiveness. The past is the past, and God has now set me on a new path. He has allowed me to close out the poorly written chapters of my life and offered me the astonishing opportunity to write a better ending. I now have joy as I patiently await His continually unfolding plan for me. Each day brings a new surprise. Each day brings another opportunity. Each day brings me closer to the man God made me to be. And each day, my responsibility is continues to be willing to make that next good choice.

What About You? Do you feel stuck in the present because of bad choices you have made in your past? It does not have to be that way. You can choose to not allow your past choices to define who you are. That is a burden none of us need carry. God is a big, big God, and if you are ready and willing to step past your past and into a new life, He is there for you. Allow Him to help you strengthen a new mindset of no more squandering.

Encouraging Words: Proverbs 5:9-14; 2 Corinthians 6:1; James 4:14; Ephesians 5:16-17

3 A.M. FRIENDS

Too often we underestimate the power of a touch, a smile, a kind word,
a listening ear, an honest compliment, or the smallest act of caring,
all of which have the potential to turn a life around.
~ Leo Buscaglia[61]

A heart is crying out for help at the most inopportune time. It is in deep pain and despair, and there are valid reasons. But that is not the point. The point is, who is going to show up, stand up, and point up, regardless of the inconvenience, for that hurting heart? I am pretty sure it's it will be a 3 a.m. friend.

Scenario: A young couple with two young children must constantly scratch and claw to make ends meet. The washing machine unceremoniously ceases to work in the middle of the first load of the weekend wash. Through Craigslist, they find a replacement nearby and manage to get the machine home. Neither knows a thing about tools, home repairs, or maintenance, and so their hope now is that a 3 a.m. friend can come to show them how to disconnect the old and hook up the new.

Scenario: They are both well into their seventies. What had been hoped to be a pleasant winter season of their life together is anything but that. While he's he has had his share of medical issues—older age annoyances, as he prefers to call them—she is being progressively in the early throes of being claimed by the cruel, relentless tentacles of dementia and elder depression. Because of their financial situation he has been thrust into the unanticipated role of full-time caretaker for his wife and often feels as if he is in a living hell. What family there is consists of those who only help occasionally, those who are far away but

111

want to help, and those who are blinded by the reality of the situation and do not want to help. Lacking a 3 a.m. friend or two will eventually spell trouble for gramps as he heads toward crash and burn for trying to exceed his own capabilities in the situation he is facing.

So, what is such a friend, this 3 a.m. friend? Who are they? Why are they the way they are? Where do they come from?

A 3 a.m. friend is not that friend who answers your drunk call at 3 a.m., though they could be have been to some. Rather, they are the folks out there with the biggest hearts—for others. They value others. They are in it because that's how they are wired. They see things differently, and they are attuned to others' needs, whether asked or not. They are not necessarily long-standing friends. They are simply friends who love their neighbors as, through God's grace, they've learned to love themselves.

A 3 a.m. friend will always be there when needed, and not necessarily because they were asked to be, nor because they really want to be. They are there because that is who they are. A 3 a.m. friend is humble. Often, they have faced situations where a 3 a.m. friend has been available in their time of need. Many 3 a.m. friends know the power of paying it forward. They are not looking for recognition or affirmation. That is not what love for others seeks.

About Me: As a young boy, there was an extended period when our family was poorer than dirt, so much so that there were times when my parents had no food in the house. They were people of great faith, and while they never lost hope, at times, things got tense. Invariably, some 3 a.m. friend would show up with a basket or box full of food supplies or meals. I remember times when my parents did not even know the people that showed up. Those folks had simply heard from a friend of a friend that we were having troubles.

On an uglier note, I remember vividly the twenty- to thirty-year span of my life when I was "in my cups." I was a very adept practicing drunk. During that time, if I was in a particularly bad place mentally and emotionally, I would periodically make quite disturbing drunk calls in the wee hours of the morning to a couple of folks who I later realized were truly 3 a.m. friends, figuratively and literally. They would sometimes call me back within a day or two to check up on me. They would often use that time to lovingly try to get through to me while I was in a better state of mind. The point is, they never gave up on me, defiled me, chastised me. They only loved on me and prayed for me.

As my heart began to change over the years, I came to see how big a role "love your neighbor" had played in my life. I gained insight into how through compassion, empathy, awareness, and action I could humbly love my own neighbor as myself and reach out to the hurting. Even at inconvenient times, with unpleasant circumstances and when my head was screaming no, I knew I had to be that 3 a.m. friend. In my current enlightened frame of mind, I heartily embrace the fact that it is the Jesus way of doing life.

What About You? Do you tend to see the needs of others as issues of inconvenience or through 3 a.m. eyes? How are you at anticipating or sensing needs in others that are all too often not openly expressed? It may take rethinking priorities and rearranging your comfortable schedule, but you can be a blessing and be personally blessed as you demonstrate love to your neighbor at 3 a.m. (or, of course, any other time).

Encouraging words: Mark 12:31; Matthew 22:36-40; John 15:12; 1 John 4:21; Romans 13:10; Leviticus 19:34

SISSIES

It's about how hard you can get hit and keep moving forward.
~ Rocky Balboa[62]

If you saw the movie *Rocky*, you saw near the end that Rocky Balboa literally had the snot beaten out of him. In true Hollywood fashion, he endured what no mortal man should have to endure, yet he kept picking himself up to continue the fight, which he ultimately won. He took it, took more, kept taking it, and kept moving forward until he won. He absolutely was no (as we used to say back in the day) sissy.

Many personalities in the Bible—Paul, Job, Joseph, Moses, Naomi, Jeremiah, David, to name a few—like Rocky, were certainly no sissies either. Throughout their individual lives, they just kept taking it, whatever was served up to them. Each of their stories is filled with adversity or some horrendous treatment or dire circumstances, yet even while tempted to quit at times, they kept moving forward. Ultimately, God revealed His plan for their lives, and each met their reward.

We are no different than any of those characters in that God has given us life and has His plan for each of us. There is nothing in the Bible that tells us life will be beautiful, easy, fair, or just—though many of us think that it should be. There is nothing in the Bible that says we will not be knocked off our feet, have the snot beaten out of us (by life), be tempted mightily, or lose everything we hold dear. Basically, we are simply reassured that God has a plan for each of us.

About Me and You: We do have options when life does not go our way. We can take it, and take it, and take it some more, and eventually rise above it and win like Rocky and those in the Bible did. Or we can be sissies and quit because we think we cannot take any more. With the sissy option, we thumb our nose at God, take control ourselves, and wimp out. Yeah, sometimes life sucks, but being a sissy does as well. The better option is to acknowledge that God is in control. He has a plan for us, and we need to let His plan work. We just need to choose our option wisely. (And if you don't know those biblical personalities I mentioned, take some time to read their stories and be further encouraged.)

Encouraging Words: Proverbs 24:16

REGRETS

We all make mistakes, have struggles, and even regret things in our past.
But you are not your mistakes, you are not your struggles, and you are
here NOW with the power to shape your day and your future.
~ Steve Maraboli[63]

Regret, as a verb and as it relates to our past: to be deeply sorry for. And as a noun: sorrow which is aroused by circumstances beyond one's control or power to repair.

About Me: During an interesting discussion with a friend, the topic of regrets came up. The person was quite emphatic in expounding on how much he regretted many of the things he had done in his past. Because I know him as a godly man, his remarks surprised me. I could not shake the feeling that he was focusing too much of his attention on his past, as opposed to celebrating the beautiful man he has become, in part because of his past.

When my friend, who knows many of the sordid details of my past, asked me how I felt about my past, I shared that I did not have any regrets from it. I explained that for a good length of time, I did live with regrets, and during that time, I was an unhappy person because I was focusing on the bad me, the old me, and not the me I had become or the me I could yet become. I explained that living with regrets was, to me, like carrying a heavy and old worn suitcase that keeps opening, allowing everything to spill out. I shared my belief that God, who knew me before I was born, knew every hair on my head, and thus He was perfectly aware of the paths I would take in my life. And during my travels on those paths, some of which were certainly not nice, good, or right, I passionately believed that God's had had been all over me, just as it is now. God protected others from me, and He protected me from others. Most importantly, He protected me from me—just as He still does and always will. Because I firmly believe that God's plan for me has been a constant since before my inception, regretting my past would, in effect, be regretting God's presence in my life. Then I shared my final thought: God, the potter, has been molding me for my entire existence, and while I may not always know what He is doing, it's a sure-fire fact that He knows. For me to regret anything would be the same as thumbing my nose at God. I shared with my friend him that while I certainly wasn't happy about the bad things I have done in the past, I can look at them as lessons learned during the course of growing up spiritually, something that bodes well in transparently presenting myself as an example of what God can do with a lump of clay.

By having faith in the true power of what God's grace means for all of us, none of us need be bound by regrets over our past.

What About You? If you are carrying a suitcase full of regrets, might the weight of it be limiting the you that you can be? Setting aside that suitcase will better enable you to re-evaluate and appreciate how God has been working in your life. Do not forget that your past defines you only if you allow it. You are the you of today.

Encouraging Words: Philippians 3:13

SECRETS

Lukewarm people don't really want to be saved from their sin;
they want only to be saved from the penalty of their sin.
~ Francis Chan[64]

The best kept secret is one we all have. Although we like to think it is a secret, and we try to maintain it as one, we can't. We try to hide it. We tend not to share it. We are embarrassed by it. And we think others will look at us in a different light if we are open about it. We may think that if we ignore it, it will just go away. So, what is this secret? It is our sin.

Being transparent and open is tough. Because we are trying to publicly live as Christians in an often-contentious world, we feel acknowledging any sin will somehow stain us or shame us. What will my friends think of me?

Let's step back to basics. God knows our sin. He knows it before we do it. He loves us despite our sin, but He does hate our sin. Sin is about spiritual warfare, yet there is no need to hide if we understand that we can win the battles within that war. How do we do that?

- Never cease praying about our sin.
- Keep in the Word, where we can find an abundance of counsel.
- Participate in a trust-laden small group and share with regular transparency about our sin.
- Know that secrets kept are far more damaging to our spiritual growth than not facing them.
- Help others in their sin struggles as a means of helping yourself in yours.

- Focus on the full measure of God's amazing love and the bounty of His abundant grace.

Spiritual growth comes from sharing secrets, not from holding onto them.

About Me: The "when the rubber meets the road" moment for me came when I finally grasped that I lacked integrity because of my secret sin something I had wrongly rationalized and somehow felt I had justified. In that moment, it became crystal clear that I was at the crossroads of dying to my sin or dying with my sin. I could no longer pretend to be a godly man. It was either/or. Though it hurt and was embarrassing, when I released the secret in a God-honoring way, I found healing and freedom such that I had never experienced before. It was then that real spiritual growth began in my life.

What About You? Are there secrets that are standing in the way of your spiritual growth? How are those secrets preventing you from being the best person you can be, a truly godly person? A full appreciation of God's grace, grace which He extends to all of us, can help you make the choice to step out of your sin and into His light.

Encouraging Words: 1 John 1:8-10; Romans 3:23; 1 Corinthians 10:13; Ecclesiastes 7:20

MY JOB

During our lives, most of us will have at least one primary job through which we earn the income necessary to provide for ourselves and our family. It is not uncommon for some to hold secondary jobs to augment income to provide for families or to enjoy some of life's perks. Regardless of the work we did or still do, however, we each have a job that truly impacts how we live our daily lives. I choose to call it our life job. It is entirely different than our avocation in that our life job will always transcend that avocation. Our life job is managing our boundaries to prevent doorways to unwanted chaos, drama, fear, or failure from opening and interrupting our joy and peace. Following is how I define my life job:

It is not my job to fix others.
It is my job to fix myself and my own brokenness or inadequacies.
It is not my job to get unduly or erroneously angry with others.
It is my job to be okay when someone gets angry with me.
It is not my job to take responsibility for others' issues.
It is my job to care for and help others when I can.
It is not my job to depend on others for my happiness.
It is my job to make myself happy the godly way.
It is not my job to try to please everybody.
It is not my job to have to agree with everyone.
It is my job to know that everyone does not always have to
agree with me.
It is my job to freely understand and own my own feelings.
It is my job to be sensitive to the feelings of others.

It is my job to love others without discrimination or judgment.
It is my job to forgive when I'm discriminated against or judged.
It is my job to know what I am, and to know that I am enough.

The more we focus on how we perceive others think of us, the less reliant we are on the grace that God has extended to others and to us. When we allow our sense of sufficiency to be derived from the opinions of others and from the things of the world, we are basically living with a lack of appreciation for the sufficiency of Christ and the impact that should have on our lives. Once our boundaries are filtered strictly through a reliance on Christ and a solid understanding of God's grace, we know without a doubt that the most important job we have is to be a devoted follower of Christ—and, trust me, it won't even feel like a job!

Encouraging Words: 2 Corinthians 3:5; 2 Corinthians 12:9; Philippians 4:13; 2 Timothy 1:7

WE'RE ALL AUTHORS

We are each the authors of our own lives, Emma.
We live in what we have created.
There is no way to shift the blame
and no one else to accept the accolades.
~ Barbara Taylor[65]

I am a writer. I have published a book. And when I was writing song lyrics, one of my songs was published. This has all occurred in the later stages of my life. It surely was not something that I had planned on earlier in life. It just happened. The first book I wrote—today, I'd say that I was wearing my writer's diapers when I wrote it. The song—it never made the charts, but it got published. The point is, even later in life, I was able to discover a new and fulfilling purpose and passion in life: writing. Ironically, over the years, I had been told something that countless people have heard, perhaps you as well: "You should write a book." Typically, when that was said to me, I sensed that it was usually because people thought I could create a best seller based on the dysfunctional way I lived my life.

Truthfully, we are all authors. We are each writing a book, perhaps titled: *My Book of Life*. Each new day we are given a new page on which to write. We are free to choose what goes on that page, free to put on it whatever we want. God gave all of us free choice, and it is the daily choices we make that get written on each page of our book of life. It would create some fascinating reading, wouldn't you say?

About Me: Realizing that my clock is ticking away, I feel very blessed to know that the time will come when I will have the opportunity to hear God say the words, "Well done, my son." Awaiting those words provides me the incentive I need to keep on writing well. Not earthly books and songs, but my own book of life. Though the earlier chapters of my book weren't always of a God-honoring lifestyle, I have faith that God will be smiling as He reads the latter chapters because it's from Him that I learned all that I would eventually write in them.

What About You? How does your book of life read? As you write each daily page, have you thought how your story will finish? I pray that your book of life will be a personal best seller with an incredibly happy ending.

Encouraging Words: Matthew 25:14-30; Hebrews 11:6

GOD AND HUMOR

I had a passing thought. I wondered if God might have been drunk
when He created me. Then it dawned on me—of course not.
He was just God being God, and He knew exactly what He was doing
and what the outcome would be.
~ Joe Miller

I have a difficult time being around Christians who seem devoid of a sense of humor, especially as I get to know them and there is no change. You know the kind I am talking about: poker faced with no laughter or smile lines on their face, stern looking, pursed lips, stiff, permanently intense eyes with little life in them. From their countenance, you might think them judgmental or puritanical. They seem uncomfortable around anyone who is not like them, and sometimes conversations with them are difficult, both to start and to maintain. When I am around a person like that, it's not unusual for me to get the feeling that they are looking right through me, and I find that creepy. Because I sense that I must be on guard, engaging with them becomes forced. I, with my weird sense of humor, think of them as modern-day Pharisees. Please do not get me wrong—I'm completely aware that a single connection (or even a string of them) with a person exhibiting those characteristics is not conclusive proof that they are as described above. Understandably, not all folks are going to be happy Harrys, especially if they have recently suffered some catastrophic adversity. I am not talking about those people. I am talking about the people who comport themselves as such for a living, on an everyday basis.

I'm sure God had a wicked sense of humor. I think that He named the animal called a dog, dog, because it is God spelled backwards and they do constantly display so many of His wonderful attributes. They are, thus, His daily reminders to pet lovers like me, who needs constant reminders, to be more like Him. ~ Joe Miller

We humans, I believe, are supposed to have a sense of humor. A good sense of humor. Humor which is funny without being at the expense of anyone or anything. Humor that is not hurtful, bathed in sin, or blasphemous in any way. Often, the best possible humor we can share is when we poke fun at ourselves.

Since we are told that we are made in God's image, couldn't we rightfully assume that perhaps God Himself has a sense of humor? Is that a horrifying thought? Is it cringeworthy? Does the thought possibly shatter a long-held mental image of God—one in which He is pictured as stern, harsh yet loving, and completely stoic—kind of like the Iowa folks pictured in the famous *American Gothic* painting by Grant Woods? Does the thought of God laughing, or chuckling make you gasp in indignation?

I think perhaps we humans tend to use ourselves as the benchmark when we either embrace or reject the concept of God having a sense of humor. I think that is a skewed comparison because God, being pure, would create or engage in nothing but pure laughter and humor. The Bible, *God's inspired Word*, is full of examples of humor, and I'm sure that God *wanted* that humor included, which to me indicates that He has a sense of humor. As my friend Irv says, *"Of course, God has a sense of humor. Who else would have made giraffes and dodo birds?"*

I look at the story of the Ark of the Covenant in the book of Samuel, and I can just picture God chuckling as He poked at the Philistines. It may be dry wit, but it is humorous. Check it out.

In the story of Jonah, I can almost picture God laughing at Jonah and saying something like, "Come on, man!" after Jonah's escapades. Check it out.

How about the foot race when John beat Peter to the empty tomb? Or Peter's gusto in much of what he did? I can pretty much picture God shaking His head saying, "Boys, settle down!" as He chuckled. Check them out.

The story of Moses and Aaron and the Golden Calf is an early example of humor, and a classic one at that. Check it out.

The story of Balaam and the talking donkey in the Old Testament is funny. God had to be rolling on the floor over that one. Check it out.

Peter walking on water was as funny as me trying to dance. Check it out.

Most of this book is quite serious, of necessity—because the subject matter of living life the Christian way is nothing to mess around with. Lives and salvation are a serious matter, just as godly relationships are. But that does not mean we have to take ourselves so seriously all the time. We can, and should, lighten up occasionally, if for no other reason than for our emotional well-being and mental health. Humor and laughter are often great medicines which we should not neglect. Based on that, the balance of this article is for you—a little "light-time." Get loose, lighten up, and carry a smile for a while. Enjoy!

(The following thoughts are to be attributed to me, Joe Miller, and my perhaps somewhat weird sense of humor.)

I sort of like how God gave us that big book of rules (for living) and essentially said, "Now figure it out." I've been cramming for my finals ever since I picked it up.

Sometimes, when I screw up, I can see clearly in my mind: there God is, sitting on His throne next to Jesus, and He nudges Jesus, leans over, and says, "Look at that." Then He shakes His head and says, "Joey, Joey, Joey, will you ever get it?"

It's not uncommon for me to think with a high degree of certainty that He just asked me, "What part of no don't you understand, son?"

Do you ever wonder if there are times when He just shouts out, "Hey, I'm the boss here"?

I'm a piece of work. I think that must be why God took the seventh day off. I'm pretty sure I was a project on which He had to put in overtime to get the job done and He was tired.

God and my mom had something in common. I've heard them both say, "If I told you once, I told you a thousand times."

In my younger years, I was convinced that God had size 83½ EEEE shoes and one leg was lifted to stomp me at any moment. Now I realize just how much He loves me, because what He was actually stomping was whatever He wanted to keep me from getting into next.

Sometimes, I think God has right by His throne this little red "feel bad" button that is somehow hooked up to my head and heart, because when I mess up bad and don't have second thoughts within a set period of time, I'm pretty sure that's when He pushes it so I'll start to realize I should be remorseful about what I just did. I'm a little slow sometimes.

I like to think that when I have those times when I'm centered in Him, focused on my spiritual life, and in general, when my head and heart are in sync, that He's up there kind of smiling as He's bragging, "Yup, that feller, I made him, and he's come a long way."

The more that time passes in my Christian walk, I find that the more I know I know, the more I don't know. And the more I don't know, the more perplexing it is to know that I don't know what I don't know. Knowing that I don't know what I don't know becomes a bit of a challenge in itself. Kind of makes my head want to explode sometimes.

Sometimes, when I get down on myself because I'm having trouble running the affairs of daily life, I just have to stop and catch a breath and remind myself, "Dude—chill out. That guy, God, He's running the whole universe. What are you whining for?"

I've often wondered if the two skunks on the Ark ever let it loose.

I've lusted in my lifetime, as have many I know. Perhaps you have. I wonder if animals lust. I don't think so. I think we are the only ones, thanks to that couple in the garden.

LIFE SOMETIMES SUCKS

When you find your path, you must not be afraid.
You need to have sufficient courage to make mistakes.
Disappointment, defeat, and despair
are the tools God uses to show us the way.
~ Paulo Coelho[66]

Life. Sometimes, it just sucks.
Disappointment, one of our more disturbing emotions, dances in our heads like a fine ballet. It lounges around casually but prominently in the front of our minds, while feeling like the ghost that won't go away in the back of our minds. And it tends to paint our inner thoughts a dreadful shade of gray.

We experience disappointment because we feel that someone, something, or perhaps we ourselves, has let us down. And in those times of disappointment, we will sometimes hear supposed wise words of wisdom: "Suck it up, baby. Time to put those big-boy pants on." Even if we do not hear the actual words, we get the impression that those verbal gems are what someone wants to say to us. Maybe we hear the voices in our own heads speak those words. But we seldom listen. And if we do listen, that does not stop the our disappointment dance, does it? So, what will?

I suggest four disappointment dance stoppers: **S-L-A-P.**

Shift from "Why me?" to "What's next?"
Whenever something goes haywire or sideways in our life, the natural response is often "Why me?" It is all too easy to think like the victim

128

we want to be at the time, and that, of course, helps us to feel incompetent about dealing with a situation. When we start to go down that mental pathway, we need to replace it with "What's next?" This puts us in the driver's seat and helps us sort out what to do next.

Learn from the Experience

If open to learning, we just may discover that the situation which produced the disappointment is not really as it seemed, and the disappointment is just a molehill rather than the mountain we envisioned it to be. When we are thinking that no good can come from the situation, ask some questions: What am I misreading about this situation? How can I approach a reaction of disappointment differently in the future? In other words, we need to focus on what we can learn from the situation.

Accept Imperfection

Disappointments almost always revolve around people (yup, us humans) in some manner. Oops, none of us are perfect. And none of us are humanly able to get it right all the time. Our best option is to go gently with the flow and look for ways to improve rather than perfect. By accepting that there can be imperfections, we open the door to explore improvement possibilities without the added stress of frustration and disappointment.

Practice Gratitude

It almost seems laughable to try to feel grateful amid one of those life really sucks moments. Hence, the keyword: Practice. We usually tend to reserve gratitude for those more reflective moments in our lives. However, in whatever situation caused the disappointment, we need to look for a silver lining (it may be just a tiny one—but there will be one) and be grateful for that—*out loud!* If we practice gratitude each time the disappointment dance begins, it just might become a habit, and we just might find ourselves doing the happy dance instead.

LIFE'S CROSSROADS

Today I choose life. Every morning when I wake up,
I can choose joy, happiness, negativity, pain.
To feel the freedom that comes from being able to continue
to make mistakes and choices—today I choose to feel life,
not to deny my humanity but embrace it.
~ Kevyn Aucoin[67]

Many of us live in prisons of sorts. Some of those prisons are nicer than others, and some are far worse. That said, our focus need not be on that which constrains or restricts us, but rather on our attitudes, actions, and beliefs despite those constraints and restrictions. It is our faith which defines us, not our prisons. Paul, the most prolific writer in the New Testament, speaks often of prisons, both literally and figuratively. He is as open about his personal demons (prisons) as he is about the persecutions against him, which included multiple imprisonments. Through it all, he always stayed true to God whenever he came to a crossroad. Paul's many writings in Scripture reflect that, just as they provide a plethora of lessons each of us can follow. Reading and reflecting on Paul's writings will shed light on how we can react in a godly way when we reach one of life's crossroads. Instead of just selective verses, a list of this prolific writer's books can be found under Encouraging Words.

About Me: I've often referred to my life as traveling on a long dirt road. Though I know my destination, my experiences tell me that whatever distance is left will not be all smooth traveling. Despite my best efforts, there are sure to be curves, mountains to climb, valleys to traverse, and roadblocks to negotiate. Easy street, freeway traveling, and a fun road trip are often only pleasurable figments of my imagination. I embrace my walk of life as a challenge and work, and I know deep inside that at times it will require painful decisions. It teaches me specific, necessary, and sometimes painful things about myself that I need to learn. I'm sure that won't change, and I really wouldn't want it any other way. As an analogy, I sometimes see myself as a prisoner held captive by circumstances (both in and out of my control), life's vagaries, thoughts, my own missteps, and yes, even my need to change. Often, in my mind, that prison is not as nice as I would want it to be.

What I have come to appreciate about that prison is that it invariably leads me to crossroads where I have opportunities to make choices (wise or unwise) that determine how I react to whatever the current circumstance/s might be. When I focus on the wise choice, I find it often prompts me to practice the faith I talk about far more eloquently than I sometimes practice it. It is at that point that the prison which I had perceived becomes what it really is, a great blessing. The more I learn and experience this, the more I am convinced that I build my prisons in my mind and not my heart. The heart releases me from them.

What About You? Do you feel at times that you are being held captive in a prison? What do you focus on during those times? Are your prisons testing your faith or building it? As you come to any crossroads in your life, know that the discomfort you may have experienced in getting there wanes in comparison to the feeling of freedom that comes with making the right choices once there. You too can then expect a "get out of jail free" card.

Encouraging Words: Galatians; 1 & 2 Thessalonians; 1 & 2 Corinthians; Romans; Ephesians; Philippians; Colossians; Philemon; 1 & 2 Timothy; Titus

PERFECTLY POSITIVE

About Us: Throughout this book, there have been many instances when brokenness or weakness has been mentioned. There have also been musings about shortcomings and failures, mistakes, and sin. Reality is that no one is immune from any of those negatives. Negative truths can be factors in each of our lives no matter where our Christian walk takes us at any given time.

Hopefully, the musings offered some counteracting positive aspect of the subject matter and some encouraging words/offerings from Scripture for further study. In closing this book out, I want to share some absolute and perfectly positive truths we should always embrace with whole heart and mind as we continue our journey to the end. The truths apply equally to each of us, just as the negatives mentioned earlier do. But there is a difference. The negative truths can tear us down. The positive truths <u>will</u> build us up. As you do life, cherish, and believe these truths:

You are a child of God.
God knew you before you were born.
You are wondrously made.
You matter to God.
God loves you so much.
God will never leave you nor forsake you.
God has never broken His word and never will.
God chose you.
God's Son, Jesus, died on the cross for your sin.
God's Son, Jesus, gave His life so that you could be saved.

God's Holy Spirit lives in you.
God's Holy Spirit works in you and through you.

Encouraging Words: The Bible

A FINAL THOUGHT

I t is my prayer that you have found something of value in your personal walk toward spiritual growth and maturity. One final thought:

LIVE YOUR EULOGY

Do it day by day, every day. Do not wait for when you are in that box and someone else shares how *they* think your eulogy should read. <u>You</u> live it now. It is the Jesus way.

> *You are powerful beyond measure! Sometimes we are too afraid of what we might become so we hold on to the story we sold ourselves. You were born chosen and blessed. When you move away from stress and worry, you can begin to cultivate the greatness within. You've gotten glimpses of what you can be because of the hand of God on your life. Let's move from sickness to success. Rewrite your story and you win!!*
> ~ Kierra C. T. Banks[68]

ENDNOTES

1   Stefan Kanfer, *Groucho Marx, The Essential Groucho: Writings for, by, and about Groucho Marx* (New York, NY: Vintage Books, 2000).

2   Frederick Buechner, *Telling Secrets* (San Francisco, CA: HarperOne, 2000).

3   John Kirvan, *Let Nothing Disturb You: 30 Days with a Great Spiritual Teacher* (Notre Dame, IN: Ave Maria Press, 2008).

4   John Piper, *The Pleasures of God: Meditations on God's Delight in Being God.* (New York, NY: The Crown Publishing Group, 2000).

5   Ashleigh Slater, *Team Us: Marriage Together* (Chicago, IL: Moody Publishers, 2014).

6   Ravi Zacharias, *I, Isaac, Take Thee Rebekah: Moving from Romance to Lasting Love* (Nashville, TN: Thomas Nelson, 2005).

7   George Bernard Shaw, *Getting Married: Press Cuttings* (London, England: Penguin Books, 1990).

8   Mitch Alborn, *Tuesdays with Morrie* (Anderson, IN: Warner, 2000).

9   Jacob M. Braude and Glenn Van Ekeren, *Baude's Treasury of Wit and Humor for All Occasions* (Upper Saddle River, NJ: Prentice Hall, 1991).

10 Trent Shelton and Baylor Barbee, *You're Perfect: for the Heart That's Meant to Love You* (Kindle Book) (Ft. Worth, TX: Rehab Time Org., 2013).

11   *The Shawshank Redemption*, directed by Frank Darabont (1994; Beverly Hills, CA: Castle Rock Entertainment, 1995), Video.

12   *The Shawshank Redemption*, directed by Frank Darabont (1994; Beverly Hills, CA: Castle Rock Entertainment, 1995), Video.

13   Jonathan Anthony Burkett, *Neglected but Undefeated* (Miramar, FL: Upstormed, 2008).

14   Helen Keller, "In Behalf of the IWW (*The Liberator,* 1918)," The Human Trafficking Institute, April 14, 2020, https//www.traffickinginstitute.org/incontext-helen-keller/.

15   Cheryl Hughes, *Truth and Objectivity in Social Ethics* (Charlottesville, VA: Philosophy Documentation Center, 2003).

16   Mary Manin Morrissey, *Building Your Field of Dreams* (New York, NY: Bantam Books, 1997).

17   Fred Rogers, *The World According to Mister Rogers: Important Things to Remember* (New York, NY: Hatchette Books, 2003).

18   Oprah Winfrey, *What I Know for Sure* (New York, NY: Flatiron Books, 2014).

19   D. B. Harrop, *Pierce Ackles and the Leather Apron: The Tale of Jack the Ripper* (Bloomington, IN: Authorhouse Publishing, 2012).

20   Roy T. Bennett, *Light in the Heart* (Seattle, WA, Kindle Books) (Roy T. Bennet, 2016).

21   Lauren Oliver, *Before I Fall* (New York, NY: Harper Collins, 2010).

22   Mother Teresa and Jose Luis Gonzalez-Balado, *In My Own Words* (London, England: Hodder & Stoughton Religious, 1996).

23   *The reason why so many are still troubled, still seeking, still making so little forward progress is because they haven't yet come to the end of themselves. We're still trying to give orders and interfering with God's work within us.* ~ A. W. Tozer (https://www.goodreads.com/author/show/1082290.A_W_Tozer)

24 C. S. Lewis, *Essay on Forgiveness* (New York, NY: Macmillan Publishing, 1960).

25 Jeanette Winterson, *Oranges Are Not the Only Fruit* (London, England: Grove Press, 1997).

26 Ann Landers, *A Collection of My Favorite Gems of the Day* (Chicago, IL: Esther P. Lederer, 1994).

27 Albert Pike, *Morals and Dogma (Illustrated)* (Kindle) (London, England: Global Grey, 2013).

28 Pearl S. Buck, *The Good Earth (House of Earth 1)* (West Monroe, LA: Howard Publishing, 2009).

29 Soren Kierkegaard, Victor Eremita (Editor), and Alastair Hannay (Translator, Introduction), *Either/Or: A Fragment of Life* (London, England: Penguin Classics, 1992).

30 Steven Furtick, *Sun Stand Still* (Colorado Springs, CO: Multnomah Books, 2010).

31 John Piper, *Don't Waste Your Life* (Wheaton, IL: Crossway Books, 2003).

32 Andrena Sawyer, "As believers, our reaction to crisis reveals our heart toward God," Goodreads, date of access, 9//24/2019, https://www.goodreads.com/quotes/search?utf8=%E2%9C%93&q=andrena+Sawyer&commit=Search.

33 Timothy J. Keller and Kathy Keller, *The Meaning of Marriage: Facing the Complexities of Commitment with the Wisdom of God* (New York, NY: Dutton Adult, 2011).

34 Francis Chan, *Crazy Love: Overwhelmed by a Relentless Love* (Elgin, IL: David C. Cook, 2008).

35 John Ortberg, *The Me I Want to Be: Becoming God's Best Version of You* (Grand Rapids, MI: Zondervan Press, 2009).

36 Andrew Chong, "Spiritual maturity is not how much of the Bible you think you know..." Goodreads, date of access, 7/16/2019 https://

www.goodreads.com/quotes/search?utf8=%E2%9C%93&q=An-drew+Chong&commit=Search.

37   Criss Jami, *Healology* (Scotts Valley, CA: CreateSpace, 2016).

38   Suzy Kassem, *Rise Up and Salute the Sun: The Writings of Suzy Kassem* (Toronto, Ontario: Awakened Press, 2011).

39   Clay Shirky, *Here Comes Everybody: The Power of Organizing without Organizations* (London, England: Penguin Press, 2008).

40   Marc Maron, *Attempting Normal* (New York, NY: Spiegel and Grau, 2013).

41   Shannon L. Alder, "An open Facebook page is simply a psychiatric dry erase board..." Goodreads, date of access, 9/29/2019

42   https://www.goodreads.com/author/show/1391130. Shannon_L_Alder.

43   Marie Sarantakis, "If you don't like pictures of animal cruelty..." Goodreads, date of access, 9/29/2019 https://www.goodreads. com/author/quotes/6113896.Marie_Sarantakis.

44   Mark Manson, *The Subtle Art of Not Giving a F*ck: A Counterintuitive Approach to Living a Good Life* (San Francisco, CA: HarperOne, 2016).

45   Cal Newport, *The Digital Minimalism: Choosing a Focused Life in a Noisy World* (New York, NY: Portfolio Press, 2019).

46   Ryan Holiday, *Ego Is the Enemy: The Fight to Master Our Greatest Opponent* (London, England: Profile Books, 2017).

47   Germany Kent, *You Are What You Tweet: Harness the Power of Twitter to Create a Happier, Healthier Life* (Culver City, CA: Star Stone Press, 2015).

48   Criss Jami, *Healology* (Scotts Valley, CA: CreateSpace Independent Publishing Platform, 2016).

49   Paul Washer, *The Gospel Call and True Conversion (Recovering the Gospel)* (Grand Rapids, MI: Reformation Heritage Books, 2013).

50   Sheri L. Dew, *Saying It Like It Is* (Salt Lake City, UT: Shadow Mountain, 2009).

51   Ralph Waldo Emerson, *Nature* (London, England: Penguin Books, 2008).

52   Sue Augustine, *When Your Past Is Hurting Your Present: Getting beyond Fears That Hold You Back* (Eugene, OR: Harvest House Publishers, 2005).

53   Bob Goff, *Love Does: Discover a Secretly Incredible Life in an Ordinary World* (Nashville, TN: Thomas Nelson, 2012).

54   Beth Moore, *When Godly People Do Ungodly Things—Bible Study Book: Arming Yourself in the Age of Seduction* (Nashville, TN: Lifeway Church Resources, 2003).

55   John R. W. Stott, *Basic Christianity* (Downers Grove, IL: IVP Books, 2006).

56   Gayle Forman, *If I Stay* (New York, NY: Speak, 2010).

57   Steve Maraboli, *Unapologetically You: Reflections on Life and the Human Experience* (Port Washington, NY: A Better Today Publishing, 2013).

58   Johann Wolfgang von Goethe, *Sketchy, Doubtful, Incomplete Jottings* (London, England: Penguin Classics, 2015).

59   Isrealmore Ayivor, *The Great Hand Book of Quotes* (Scotts Valley, CA: CreateSpace Independent Publishing Platform, 2014).

60   Francis Chan, *Crazy Love: Overwhelmed by a Relentless Love* (Elgin, IL: David C. Cook, 2008).

61   Gordon B. Hinkley, *The Essence of True Religion* (Salt Lake City, UT: Shadow Mountain, 1989).

62 Leo Buscaglia, *Loving Each Other* (New York, NY: Ballantine Books, 1986).

63 *Rocky Balboa*, directed by Sylvester Stallone (2006; Los Angeles, CA: Revolution Studios, 2007), Blu-ray and DVD.

64 Steve Maraboli, *Unapologetically You: Reflections on Life and the Human Experience* (Port Washington, NY: A Better Today Publishing, 2013).

65 Francis Chan, *Crazy Love; Overwhelmed by a Relentless Love* (Elgin, IL: David C. Cook, 2008).

66 Barbara Taylor Bradford, *A Woman of Substance* (Spokane, WA: Griffin Publishing, 2005).

67 Paulo Coelho, *Brida* (San Francisco, CA: HarperOne, 2009).

68 Kevyn Aucoin, "Today, I choose life..." Goodreads, date of access, 11/12/2019 https://www.goodreads.com/quotes/search?utf8=%E2%9C%93&q=Kevyn+Aucoin&commit=Search.

Thank you for reading Dog Walk Talk.
I pray that you are taking something good from it,
for you, as you continue your life's journey.

You can see my third book unfolding on my website
www.jbmillerauthor.com